BEATING OBAMACARE
2014

BEATING
OBAMACARE
2014

Avoid the Landmines and Protect
Your Health, Income, and Freedom

BETSY McCAUGHEY, Ph.D.

REGNERY
Publishing, Inc.
Washington, DC • Since 1947

Cataloging-in-Publication data on file with the Library of Congress
ISBN 978-1-62157-242-8

Published in the United States by
Regnery Publishing, Inc.
One Massachusetts Avenue NW
Washington, DC 20001
www.Regnery.com

This is the second Regnery edition, published in 2014
First Regnery edition published in 2013 as *Beating Obamacare*,
ISBN 978-1-62157-079-0

Some material in this book appeared previously in electronic form in the ebook *Decoding the Obama Health Law: What You Need to Know* published in 2012 by Paperless Publishing LLC, 609 Greenwich Street, New York, NY 10014.

Manufactured in the United States of America

10 9 8 7 6 5 4 3 2 1

Books are available in quantity for promotional or premium use. Write to Director of Special Sales, Regnery Publishing, Inc., One Massachusetts Avenue NW, Washington, DC 20001, for information on discounts and terms or call (202) 216-0600.

Distributed to the trade by
Perseus Distribution
250 West 57th Street
New York, NY 10107

In honor of the physicians and researchers
who gave us the golden age of medicine

CONTENTS

CHAPTER ONE
Obamacare Will Change Everyone's Healthcare.................. 1

CHAPTER TWO
It's Mandatory.. 13

CHAPTER THREE
Obamacare's Substandard Exchange Plans 25

CHAPTER FOUR
What Employers and Employees Need to Know 41

CHAPTER FIVE
Paying for More Benefits You Don't Want......................... 59

CHAPTER SIX
Medicaid Nation... 65

CHAPTER SEVEN
Obamacare Raids Medicare and Hurts Seniors 73

CHAPTER EIGHT
The Tax Man Cometh 87

CHAPTER NINE
Doctors Reject Obamacare...................................... 97

CHAPTER TEN
Obamacare vs. the Rule of Law 105

CHAPTER ELEVEN
If You Like Your God, You Can Keep Your God 123

CHAPTER TWELVE
Washington's Misguided Views on Health Reform 131

CHAPTER THIRTEEN
Beating Obamacare 141

The Obamacare Calendar 151

Who Gains and Who Loses.. 159

The Obamacare Dictionary 163

Acknowledgments 193

Notes.. 197

Index.. 221

CHAPTER ONE

OBAMACARE WILL CHANGE EVERYONE'S HEALTHCARE

Facts You Need to Know:

- Millions of people will lose their on-the-job coverage
- If you already have insurance you like, it will probably be cancelled
- You'll have to show the IRS proof of insurance when you file your taxes

All across the country, doctors, hospitals, businesses, and families are taking urgent action to soften the impact of the Obama health law. You need to know what is ahead and what you can do to protect yourself, your family, and your income.

You've heard President Obama say many times, "If you like your health care plan, you will be able to keep

your health care plan. Period. No one will take it away. No matter what."[1]

That's not true. By November 1, 2013, millions of insured Americans already had received cancellation notices. All in all, most people with individual coverage they bought themselves will see it cancelled. These plans do not comply with the federal government's definition of "essential" coverage. The president has even called these existing plans "substandard" and "cut-rate."[2] (But as you'll see in Chapter Three, it's the plans on the Obamacare exchanges that are really substandard.) So be prepared. You may think you're covered and have nothing more to do. But if you have insurance you bought on the individual market, you will likely lose it and have to buy a plan in the new Obamacare exchange.

If you currently get your health insurance through a job, you may lose it. The Congressional Budget Office predicts that some employers, faced with costly new Obamacare regulations, will drop coverage altogether.[3] Only in Washington, D.C., could "health reform" result in workers losing their health insurance. According to management consultants McKinsey & Company, one-third of employers are considering dropping coverage for their employees.[4] But that doesn't mean you'll be uninsured. You won't have that choice.

When you file your taxes, you will have to show proof that you are enrolled in the one-size-fits-all plan approved by the federal government. It's mandatory. If you can't prove it, then the IRS will withhold your refund. If you've been going without coverage, or your employer dumps coverage, your options will be enrolling in Medicaid (if you're eligible) or buying a plan on the Obamacare exchange.

What is an exchange? It's like a supermarket that only sells cereal. The exchange sells only the government-designed plan. Subsidies will be available for moderate-income families.

You probably won't be able to continue using the doctors and hospitals you prefer. The vast majority of exchange plans don't allow access to top-drawer academic hospitals like Cedars-Sinai in Los Angeles or New York Presbyterian in New York City.[5] In New Hampshire, exchange plans exclude nearly half the hospitals in the state.[6]

Exchange plans are required to include hospitals that customarily serve the poor. The authors of the Affordable Care Act reasoned that exchange plan customers should be able to shift back and forth between their plans and Medicaid, as their earnings fluctuate, without changing doctors and hospitals. That's good news for them, but bad news for customers who had access to highly regarded hospitals and doctors, and now have to settle for less.

If you're a senior or a baby boomer, expect less care than in the past. Cuts to future Medicare funding will pay for more than half the Obama health law. Hospitals, for example, will have $247 billion less over a decade to care for the same number of seniors than if the law had not passed. So hospitals will spread nurses thinner. When Medicare cuts caused hospitals to reduce nursing care in the past, elderly patients had a lower chance of surviving their stay, and death rates from heart attacks rose.[7]

If you're in a Medicare Advantage plan, you've probably already received a letter telling you that your plan is dropping your doctor. UnitedHealthcare axed thousands of cardiologists and other specialists from their Advantage plans in New York and Connecticut.[8] The same thing is happening around the country because of large cuts in what the federal government pays Advantage plans.

For the first time in history, the federal government will control how doctors treat privately insured patients. Section 1311(h) of the law empowers the Secretary of Health and Human Services to standardize what doctors do. Even if you have a private plan from Cigna or Aetna and you paid for it yourself, the federal government will have some say over your doctors' decisions—with an eye to reducing healthcare consumption.

If you sell your house and make a profit, you could be paying a new 3.8 percent tax on the gain. Obamacare includes about half a trillion dollars in tax hikes. One that many people still don't know about is the 3.8 percent additional tax on gains from selling any asset, including your home, small business, stocks, or bonds, effective January 1, 2013. The new tax is on top of capital gains taxes, and it applies to any gain that pushes your income over $200,000. (Homeowners selling a primary residence may be excluded under some circumstances.)

If you're operating a business, Obamacare is providing what businesses hate most: uncertainty. The Affordable Care Act imposed numerous requirements on employer-provided health insurance that have already gone into effect. But the big issue—the employer mandate—is in limbo. Employers spent the first six months of 2013 either preparing to comply or shifting full-time workers to part-time status to avoid the burden imposed by the law. Then on July 2, 2013, the Obama administration quietly postponed the mandate.[9] Will the employer mandate ever go into effect? You'll find the answer in Chapter Four.

The Affordable Care Act has brought you something new on your W-2. Employers providing more than 250 W-2s have to report the value of employer-provided health coverage in a special Box 12. The federal government claims the reporting is for informational purposes, to help consumers see the value of their health coverage. With Washington politicians looking everywhere for new revenue—I wouldn't bank on that assurance for too long.

These are just a few of the hundreds of changes that will affect you, your family, and your job. You could wade through the 2,572-page Obama health law yourself. But if you have a better way to spend the next three months of your life, you can rely on this guide instead. It will help you understand what the law says—plus the thousands of additional regulations being written right now.

The Obama administration is adding federal workers at a rapid pace to churn out these additional regulations and enforce them. The government's own projections say healthcare administration—paying bureaucrats to tell doctors and patients what to do—will soar from the $29 billion it cost when President Obama was first elected to $71 billion by 2020.[10] Forty billion dollars a year more in bureaucracy. What a shame. And what an irony. That's enough money to buy private health plans for fully half of all Americans who are currently uninsured because they can't afford it.

Thousands of new regulations have already been written to control what you, your doctor, and your employer can do. To help you survive this avalanche of new rules, I've prepared this simple guide.

Decoding the Law

If you're clueless about the Obama health law, you're not alone. Most people have heard the political bickering and supercharged rhetoric, but they don't know what the law actually says.

But you'll need to know soon, because this law affects you and your entire family. The new health law is not just about helping the uninsured (a worthy goal). Obamacare changes how everyone in America gets medical care. It will even regulate the decisions your doctor can make. You haven't felt the effects yet, but you will.

One reason for the political rancor over this new law is that so few people—including even members of Congress—have read it. The law is 2,572 pages. Why so long? The framers of the U.S. Constitution created the entire federal government in just eighteen pages. If only the Washington bigwigs of today showed the same restraint.

In addition to the law's length, its obfuscating language gives readers the runaround. Who could understand this gobbledygook?

Here's a typical passage from the Obama health law:

(1) Subparagraph (B) of section 6724(d)(1) of the Internal Revenue Code of 1986 (relating to definitions), as amended by Section 1502, is amended by striking "or" at the end of clause

(xxiii), by striking "and" at the end of clause (xxiv) and inserting "or" and by inserting after clause (xxiv) the following new clause:

"(xxv) section 6056 (relating to returns relating to large employers required to report on health coverage), and".

(2) Paragraph (2) of section 6724(d) of such Code, as so amended, is amended by striking "or" at the end of subparagraph (FF), by striking the period at the end of subparagraph (GG) and inserting "or" and by inserting after subparagraph (GG) the following new subparagraph:

(HH) section 6056 c (relating to statements relating to large employers required to report on health insurance coverage).

The legalese you just read is from Section 6056 of the act, requiring large employers to report the insurance coverage they provide for each employee.

To even begin to comprehend this one section of the law, you'd have to consult dozens of other pieces of legislation to cobble the meaning together. Yet employers who fail to follow the provisions could face thousands of dollars of fines.

This guide decodes what the Obama health law says, and tells you, based on the Obama administration's own financial projections, how it will probably affect you. No spin, no partisanship, just a translation into plain honest English. I've read the whole unwieldy and misleading law and summarized it for you here.

Even more important, I've kept track of the myriad changes the president is making to the law, changes that will also affect you.

Obamacare Is Constantly Changing

At an October 1, 2013, press event unveiling the Healthcare.gov website, Obama brushed off critics of the healthcare law by saying "The Affordable Care Act is a law that passed the House; it passed the Senate. The Supreme Court ruled it constitutional. It was a central issue in last year's election. It is settled, and it is here to stay."[11]

Untrue, Mr. President. That claim could be made about the 2,572-page Affordable Care Act sitting on my desk. It cannot be said of Obamacare—the health program the administration rolled out in the fall of 2013. Obamacare is not the Affordable Care Act. It is a mangled, distorted version of what Congress enacted. Far from being settled law, it may not be law at all. (For more on this issue, see Chapter Ten, "Obamacare vs. the Rule of Law.")

Be aware. Obamacare is constantly changing.

At this point, it bears little resemblance to the law passed in 2010. The president has dispensed with large sections of it illegally (if you still consider the Constitution the measure). Gone is the employer mandate (probably forever). Missing are the caps on out-of-pocket expenses. Dispensed with is income verification (replaced with a limp promise in the October 2013 debt ceiling deal). Gone are over half the deadlines Congress spelled out in the statute.

Then there are the additions. President Obama added waivers for 780 companies and 451 unions[12] and weaseled a special deal making members of Congress eligible for a taxpayer-funded subsidy for their premiums, something no one else in America earning $174,000 a year could get. None of these handouts can be found in the text of the Affordable Care Act.

These illegal changes to the law create new winners and losers. Suspending the employer mandate shifts costs from employers to taxpayers. Suspending the cap on out-of-pocket expenses helps insurers but punishes the seriously ill who were initial supporters of the law.

The subsidy for members of Congress and their staff makes Washington insiders the winners and you and me the losers. We foot the bill.

But the biggest victim of these arbitrary changes is the rule of law.

You will find these changes described in detail in the chapters that follow. And this guide also tells you what you have to do to comply with the law. So let's get started. If you come across an unfamiliar word or phrase, be sure to consult the Obamacare Dictionary at the end of the guide.

Also be sure to keep a copy of the U.S. Constitution at your side. You will need it, as we consider the constitutionality of various provisions of Obamacare. If only the members of Congress had done the same, before voting to pass this law.

The prescient James Madison, chief architect of the Constitution, anticipated the danger in *The Federalist* No. 62. Madison warned that it is pointless for Americans to elect a Congress if that Congress in turn enacts laws "so voluminous that they cannot be read" or if these laws then "undergo such incessant changes that no man, who knows what the law is to-day, can guess what it will be to-morrow."[13] That is Obamacare.

CHAPTER TWO

IT'S MANDATORY

Facts You Need to Know:

- Under Obamacare, even your children are subject to penalties for being uninsured
- The IRS official responsible for targeting conservative groups has been promoted to run the IRS office in charge of your health insurance
- If you want to keep something out of your medical record, the government advises you to pay cash

P resident Obama understood that Americans didn't want big government messing with their healthcare. So when he campaigned to pass Obamacare, he told the public what they wanted to hear. He promised that "no matter how we reform health care," Americans would be able to keep the plans they already had and liked.[1] His reform would help the uninsured and leave everyone else alone. After all, 85 percent of Americans had insurance and most were happy with it.[2]

But the law the president signed on March 23, 2010, never matched up to his pledge. The fine print in that law made it impossible for most people to keep the insurance they liked.

Fast-forward to the fall of 2013. Imagine the frustration of the millions of people who got cancellation notices in the mail. People who had bought individual plans, taking care to select what they needed and could afford, were duped and dumped. Left without insurance.

Now, the same thing is beginning to happen to millions more people who get their coverage through a group plan at work. These policies have to be changed, at considerable cost. And some employers are deciding to drop coverage altogether.

The Grandfather Clause

Americans were relying on the president's promise, which he repeated publicly more than three dozen times.

"If you like your health care plan, you will be able to keep your health care plan. Period."[3]

Sounds good, but actually being able to keep their plan depended on the wording of a section of the Affordable Care Act called the grandfather clause. Section 1251(a)(1) says that no one can be required to give up a plan in effect on March 23, 2010, when the law was passed.[4] Unfortunately, the fine print allowed Obama administration regulators to impose additional requirements on grandfathered plans.

The exception was union plans, which got a separate, ironclad grandfather clause—Section 1251(d)—with no exceptions or weasel words in it.[5]

Just a few weeks after the law was signed, regulators from the IRS, the Department of Health and Human Services, and the Department of Labor—all reporting to the president—churned out numerous additional rules on grandfathered plans. The rule makers knew they were turning the president's pledge into a flimflam. In the rules, they actually forecast that most plans would not survive.

Yet even as late as September 26, 2013, literally as the cancellation notices were going into the mail, President Obama told a Maryland audience, "The first thing you need to know is this: If you already have health care, you don't have to do anything."[6]

The Individual Mandate

The individual mandate is very specific. It doesn't just require you to have health insurance. You have to have the one-size-fits-all "minimum essential coverage" designed by government experts.[7] It's like passing a law saying the only cars we are allowed to buy are four door sedans. No hatchbacks, no convertibles. The assumption is that we are too stupid to make our own choices.

Most of the policyholders who got cancellation notices in 2013 had plans that did not include "essential benefits." For example, under Obamacare rules, fifty-year-old couples have to pay for maternity care, and straight arrows have to pay for substance abuse treatment.

The individual mandate marks a milestone in our loss of liberty. For the first time, the federal government is requiring Americans to buy a product, whether you want it or not.

Where will you get it? Most Americans currently get their insurance through a job—their own job, or a spouse's, or a parent's. If you get your insurance that way, your employer is making crucial decisions right now about whether to provide the "essential benefits" and comply with all the other regulations imposed on employers, or stop offering you insurance altogether.

If you don't get your insurance through a job, or your employer dropped your coverage, you'll be enrolling in

Medicaid or buying a plan on the Obamacare exchange where you live. This guide will walk you through all those options.

On the exchanges, you'll be enrolling in a Bronze, Silver, Gold, or Platinum plan. Don't be fooled by the names. This isn't like going to Tiffany's. All these glittery-sounding plans offer the same "essential benefits" package. Only the co-pays and deductibles differ. Gold and Platinum plans make you pay more up front in your premium but allow lower co-pays and deductibles.

Just because you had health insurance doesn't mean you won't be facing these changes. Health insurance now has to conform to a government blueprint.

Penalties

When you file your taxes, you will have to attach proof that you have the government-mandated "essential coverage." You must be insured for at least ten months of the year. (Being uninsured for under three months isn't punishable.) If you fail to comply, you will have to pay the penalties illustrated below. Be aware that the fines are imposed not just on you, but also on your dependents. So by 2015, a family earning $95,000 with four children could face penalties as high as $10,500.

Penalties for Skipping Obamacare

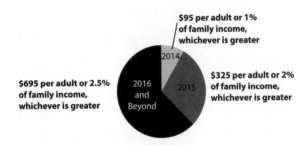

Source: IRS, "Shared Responsibility Payment for Not Maintaining Minimum Essential Coverage," *Federal Register* 78, no. 169 (August 30, 2013).

The penalties are assessed by withholding your tax refund. Many people will figure out that they can minimize their expected refund to avoid the penalty. Section 5000A(g)(2)(A) of the law expressly states that you cannot be criminally prosecuted for failing to pay the penalty.

Some groups are exempt from the mandate:

- Those who are already enrolled in government programs such as Medicare, who are considered covered
- American Indians, because they receive health insurance in a separate program and are considered covered
- Prisoners
- Members of the armed services and their families

- Certain religious groups
- Those who don't qualify for Medicaid and can prove financial hardship
- Illegal immigrants
- Young adults (under thirty) are not exempt but can meet the requirement to have a "qualified plan" by enrolling in a catastrophic insurance plan that is not available to adults thirty and over

Privacy

Most of us interact with the Internal Revenue Service once a year at tax time. But the Affordable Care Act will put many people under the IRS's thumb all the time. That's certainly true if you sign up for a health plan on the Obamacare exchange and qualify for a subsidy.

The IRS has a history of using leaks and delays to punish people based on their politics. The latest example is the news that broke in 2013 about the IRS delaying requests for tax-exempt status from conservative groups and even leaking information about them to the press.

That's frightening because the Obama health law expands the ways the IRS can hurt you. Alarmingly, the IRS official responsible for targeting conservative groups—Sarah Hall Ingram—was promoted to top dog at the IRS office in charge of your health insurance.[8]

An IRS that doesn't respect your political rights isn't likely to respect your medical privacy either. Most of us confide things to our doctor we wouldn't tell anyone else. Yet the Obama administration has pushed medical practitioners and hospitals to become part of a nationwide medical database that raises privacy concerns for patients.

Under the "meaningful use" standards imposed by the American Recovery and Reinvestment Act (stimulus legislation) of 2009, doctors and hospitals literally can't afford to keep your information private.[9] Your doctor will have to enter your treatments into an electronic database, and your doctor's decisions will be monitored for compliance with federal guidelines. Doctors and hospitals that don't comply will get whacked with penalties starting in 2015.

There is cause for concern about who sees your medical records. Mark Rothstein, a University of Louisville School of Medicine bioethicist, worries that the system will disclose too much. Rothstein warns that every doctor you see will have access to your information. Your oral surgeon doesn't need to know about your bout with depression or your erectile dysfunction but will see it.

Lack of confidentiality is what concerned the New York Civil Liberties Union in a 2012 report. Electronic medical records have enormous benefits, but with one click of a mouse, every piece of information in a patient's record, including the answers to "social history" questions such as how many sex partners you've had or whether you've ever used IV drugs, is transmitted.[10]

Yet the Department of Health and Human Services seems to ignore these protests from privacy advocates. On January 17, 2013, HHS announced that patients who want to keep something out of their electronic record should pay cash.[11] That's impractical for most people.

One important tip: defend your privacy by declining to answer the intrusive "social history" questions your doctor is being prompted to ask you to comply with federal "meaningful use" standards. The questions are embedded in software doctors are using. Many doctors consider the questions as inappropriate as you do. If you need to confide some personal information pertaining to your treatment, ask your doctor about keeping two sets of books so your secrets stay in the office. Doctors take the Hippocratic Oath seriously and won't be offended.

Paying for Your Mandatory Insurance

Obamacare creates two new entitlements to reduce the cost of mandatory insurance for some people. First, the law throws open the Medicaid doors in the twenty-six states that have chosen to implement Obamacare's Medicaid expansion.

New Entitlements under Obamacare: $1,785 Billion from 2014 to 2023

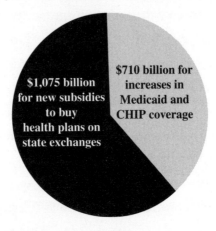

$1,075 billion for new subsidies to buy health plans on state exchanges

$710 billion for increases in Medicaid and CHIP coverage

Source: Congressional Budget Office, May 2013

President Obama often promised to solve the problem of the uninsured by making private health plans more affordable. That is not what the law does. Instead it vastly expands Medicaid, the public program for the poor. Most Americans who couldn't afford insurance are put into Medicaid. Also some low-paid workers who are currently insured on their job will soon lose that coverage and be pushed into Medicaid as well.

For more affluent households, the law creates subsidies to buy plans on the Obamacare exchanges. Generally the subsidy is paid directly to the insurer. There are no asset tests to qualify for these subsidies. You can own new cars, a home, even a castle, and still qualify. Newcomers to the

U.S. qualify for subsidies on the exchange without a waiting period, as long as they enter the country legally.

By 2019, the individual mandate and the two new entitlements will transform the healthcare landscape. According to the government's actuaries, half of all healthcare spending will be paid for by government. Of course, "paid for by government" is a myth. The new entitlements are paid for by raising our taxes and taking funds from Medicare.

The increase in government dependency, some say, will change the character of America. Families earning almost $100,000 will be getting federal subsidies or "health welfare," and millions of other Americans will be added to Medicaid, which Obamacare changes from a temporary helping hand to a permanent entitlement.

CHAPTER THREE

OBAMACARE'S SUBSTANDARD EXCHANGE PLANS

Facts You Need to Know:

- You can choose from "Bronze," "Silver," "Gold," and "Platinum" plans, but the "essential benefit" package is all the same. Only the co-pays and deductibles are different
- Only Americans under thirty can buy "catastrophic" plans
- Beware of handing a "navigator" your financial information. Unlike insurance brokers, who are background checked and fingerprinted, in most states navigators have not been vetted

Until recently, you probably had never heard of a health exchange. But if you're uninsured, or you've received a cancellation notice from your insurer, or your employer is going to drop your coverage, welcome to the exchange.

Section 1311 of the healthcare law says that each state "shall establish an American Health Benefit Exchange."[1] Only sixteen states have. Many governors and state legislatures resisted going to the expense and doing the federal government's bidding. "I'm not lifting a finger," Maine's Governor Paul LePage said. "We're going to let Mr. Obama do a federal exchange. It's his bill." LePage added that "a state exchange puts the burden onto the states and the expense onto our taxpayers, without giving the state the authority and flexibility" it needs.[2] Most governors agreed.

But nonetheless, every state has an exchange. The law says that if any state failed to set up an exchange meeting federal standards by 2013, the federal government would come in and do it. So no matter where you live, if you are uninsured, get ready to shop on the exchange.

Notice I used the word "ready." If only the exchanges had been ready for us.

The Disastrous Rollout

At 6:00 a.m. on October 1, 2013, a *New York Times* researcher began the process of registering for a health plan on the Obamacare website, www.Healthcare.gov.

Despite more than forty tries over the next eleven days, she was never able to log in, shop, and enroll. She never got beyond a blank screen.[3]

Embarrassingly, millions of other people endured the same mind-numbing experience. They were hit with frozen screens, incomprehensible directions, and endless hours of wasted time. At the end of the first day, only six people in the entire nation had managed to enroll.

The nation that developed the computer and the internet was embarrassed worldwide by its inability to launch a shop-online marketplace for health insurance. It had three and a half years to do it, but the October 1 launch collapsed.

On November 6, Secretary of Health and Human Services Kathleen Sebelius, who is responsible for implementing the Affordable Care Act, told Congress she was still working to fix "a couple of hundred" problems with the website.[4]

At that point, only four people had signed up in the entire state of Delaware, according to an Associated Press report.[5] It's a small state! Many of the state exchanges are doing no better.

All across the nation, enrollment was at a trickle. In its first month, sign-ups failed to top 106,000—vastly lower than expected.

Did cronyism play a role in the failure of the website? Perhaps. The company that got the biggest contract to set up the federal online system—CGI Federal—is a Canadian company with a lousy track record but close connections to the White House. CGI's senior vice president Toni Townes Whitley was a classmate of Michelle Obama's at Princeton, where the two were both involved in the Organization of Black Unity, the Third World Center, and other African American groups on campus.[6]

CGI was one of sixteen companies qualified to provide certain tech services to the federal government. Four of those companies submitted bids for the Healthcare.gov website work, but only CGI's was considered.[7]

A One-Size-Fits-All Plan

Brace yourself for the challenge, and eventually you will get onto the Healthcare.gov website or the website operated by your own state, such as Covered California. Depending on where you live, you'll see either just one brand listed or many. In New Hampshire, for example, only WellPoint's Anthem Blue Cross Blue Shield is offering plans on the state exchange,[8] whereas in some populous areas of the country, you may see dozens of plans listed.

You can choose from the Bronze, Silver, Gold, and Platinum versions. If only we were talking about jewelry! But far from precious metals, these are simply different levels of cost sharing. Bronze plans cover 60 percent of your medical costs, whereas Silver covers 70 percent, Gold covers 80 percent, and Platinum covers 90 percent.[9] You pay more up front to get Platinum, and then have lower co-pays and deductibles when you seek medical care.

The plans all offer the one-size-fits-all government-designed "essential benefit package."

You've heard President Obama pledge many times that under the new law, insurers would have to compete based on quality and cost, and consumers wouldn't have to worry about differences in what's covered or what the fine print says. Like comparing apples to apples. It sounds good. But keep in mind, it also means only having one choice—apples.

Another difference between a health exchange and the mall is that at the mall, you have to pay your own bill. On the exchanges, a large portion of the shoppers will be getting taxpayer-funded subsidies to help pay for their insurance. In a way, the exchange is like the health welfare store.

Here is what you need to know: your subsidy (if you can get one in your state) will be based on your household income. The subsidies will reduce the premium you actually have to pay, because taxpayers are picking up the rest of the tab. If you qualify for a subsidy, you will also have lower deductibles and lower out-of-pocket costs than someone else buying the same plan without using a subsidy.

Who Can Use the Exchanges? How Much Do You Have to Pay?

Anyone who doesn't get health insurance through Medicare, Medicaid, or an employer is eligible to shop on an exchange. Legal immigrants are not eligible for Medicaid during their first five years in the United States, but surprisingly they can shop on the exchanges and receive subsidies with no waiting period. Illegal immigrants are barred from the exchanges and free of the mandate. They are expected to get their care at federally funded community health centers.[10]

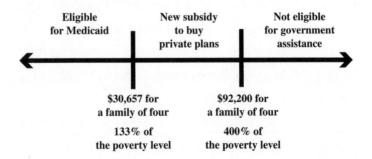

Even if your employer offers health coverage, you can shop on the exchange if you think the plan offered at work would require you to contribute more from your paycheck than you can afford. If you do enroll on the exchange, though, your employer may have to pay a $3,000 penalty for failing to offer you "affordable" coverage.

Get Ready for Sticker Shock

Despite the Affordable Care Act's name, it makes health coverage more expensive. On average, Obamacare increases premiums 41 percent, according to the Manhattan Institute's comprehensive survey. Men, the young, and the healthy get clobbered hardest.[11]

Of course, averages don't count when you're buying a plan for yourself. You need to know the facts about rates in your own location. One of the best sources is an interactive map created by the Manhattan Institute, available online at http://www.manhattan-institute.org/knowyourrates/. (Or you can just Google "Obamacare cost map.") When you are considering cost for your family, be sure to look at the deductibles as well as the premiums. On the exchanges, the deductibles are very high, about $5,000 or more per individual for a Bronze plan, and around $3,000 per individual for a Silver plan. That's about double what most employer-provided health insurance requires.

The eight states that are seeing the biggest premium increases are Nevada, up 179 percent on average; New Mexico, 142 percent; Arkansas, 138 percent; North Carolina, 136 percent; Vermont, 117 percent; Georgia, 92 percent; South Dakota, 77 percent; and Nebraska, 74 percent.[12]

Eight of the fifty states actually are seeing premiums drop: New York, Massachusetts, Colorado, Ohio, New Jersey, New Hampshire, Rhode Island, and Indiana.[13] These states already had laws similar to Obamacare's regulations—and the highest premiums in the nation as a result. Most young healthy people in these states chose not to buy insurance because it cost so much. Now that insurance is compulsory, premiums will be going down somewhat in these eight states because Obamacare forces young, healthy people to join the risk pool, lowering the average cost per person.

Under Thirty?

If you're under thirty and don't think you'll need much healthcare, the government allows you to meet the individual mandate requirement by purchasing a "catastrophic plan." The name is a bit misleading. Catastrophic health insurance generally means the kind almost everyone had two generations ago. It covered the large unexpected costs that occur when you have an accident or get rushed to the hospital with a serious illness. This "catastrophic" option, open only to the young, also includes preventive care and three visits to your primary care doctor per year.

Substandard Coverage

"Substandard" and "cut-rate" is what President Obama called the health plans that millions of Americans have lost since the fall of 2013, even though they wanted to keep them.[14] Backpedaling on his promise that "if you like your plan, you can keep your plan," Obama began telling Americans another whopper. The president claimed the insurance offered on the exchanges is better than what these Americans lost.[15]

Oops! The facts tell a different story. Many exchange plans prevent you from using the doctors and hospitals you prefer. In New Hampshire, the only insurer on the exchanges, WellPoint's Anthem Blue Cross Blue Shield, left out ten of the twenty-six hospitals in the state.[16]

In most states, the vast majority of exchange plans exclude the top drawer academic hospitals like Cedars-Sinai in Los Angeles, the Mayo Clinic in Minnesota, and New York Presbyterian in New York City.[17] The law requires that exchange plans cover care at "essential community providers…that serve predominantly low-income, medically underserved individuals" (Section 1311c(1)C).[18] That means clinics, public hospitals, and hospitals largely serving the Medicaid community.

The law's authors reasoned that exchange plan customers should be able to shift back and forth between their plans and Medicaid, as their earnings fluctuate, without changing doctors and hospitals. That's reasonable, but it's bad news for consumers who had access to esteemed hospitals and doctors under their old plans and then got pushed into the exchanges.

Medicaid-level care is, sadly, "substandard" to use the president's word. Medicaid patients get worse care than patients with private insurance.

But many of the plans being offered on the exchanges are Medicaid-like, with a private label slapped on them (Bronze, Silver, Gold, Platinum). The McKinsey Center for U.S. Health System Reform reports that Medicaid insurers are playing a large role in the exchanges.[19]

Just as many doctors refuse to accept Medicaid, they are also refusing to accept exchange insurance. In California, a Blue Cross plan on the exchange covers 47 percent fewer doctors than Blue Cross subscribers in California currently get.[20]

In New York, only a quarter of physicians have decided to take exchange insurance, because the payments are so low.[21]

Why so low? Because insurers know the low-cost plan is king in nearly every exchange. All the plans offer the "essential benefit package." As of mid-November 2013, customers had no other way to compare than on price.

That's despite the law's promise that exchanges would list each plan's quality rating and disclose which hospitals and doctors are covered (Section 1311d(4)D and Section 1311c(1)B).[22]

Why wasn't this information provided, as the law requires? We can only guess that it's because Obamacare administrators don't want us to see the truth.

The most troubling provision in Obamacare's Section 1311 gives the Secretary of Health and Human Services blanket authority to control how doctors and hospitals treat patients—all in the name of improving "quality." That could mean everything in medicine. When your cardiologist uses a stent. When your ob/gyn does a Caesarean.

What that means for you is that if you enroll in an exchange plan, with or without getting a subsidy, your care will be standardized by the federal government with an eye to reducing what you consume and how much it costs. Your doctor may have to choose between doing what's right for you and avoiding a penalty. Exchange plans can pay only those doctors who obey whatever regulations the HHS Secretary imposes.

It's hard to believe the president's claim that people who lost their health plans and had to sign up on the exchanges are getting a better deal. Losing your doctor, shopping blind for a health plan, settling for Medicaid-level care and government controls, all for a premium 41 percent higher than before and with double the deductible.[23]

Sounds substandard to me.

Beware of the Navigators

The law requires each state to set up a "navigator" program, run by non-profits, community activists, and unions. These entities—not the government—will hire and train "navigators" and "assisters" to talk up Obamacare at community events, encourage people to enroll, and walk them through the sign-up process.

Sounds good, but beware. Anyone who matches the racial and ethnic composition of the neighborhood where they're applying can qualify to be a "navigator" or "assister."

Navigators and assisters don't have to have a high school diploma, or any knowledge of math or insurance. There are no background checks to prevent ex-cons from getting the job. These precautions are standard to work for the U.S Census or the IRS, but not to be a navigator.

Navigators will have access to all your personal information—your social security number, tax returns, address, and so forth. Yikes, it's a welcome mat for identity theft.

On November 6, 2013, at a congressional hearing, Republican senator John Cornyn of Texas said to Secretary Kathleen Sebelius, "So a convicted felon could be a navigator and acquire sensitive personal information?" The Secretary replied, "That is possible."[24]

Playing Politics with the Health Exchanges

Sadly, that's only half the story. The authors of Obamacare created the navigator program as a cynical way of turning the worthy goal of enrolling the uninsured into a sneaky scheme for enrolling Democratic voters.

Why outsource the job of helping people enroll on the exchanges? Why not use government employees? Because community activists can say and do things that government employees can't, such as urging people to register to vote as Democrats.

To see how this works, look at the "Affordable Care Act Tool Kit" unveiled by House Minority Leader Nancy Pelosi, California Democrat.[25] Pelosi's kit refers users to Marc Wetherhorn, Senior Director of Advocacy and Civic Enhancement at the National Association of Community

Health Centers. Wetherhorn has developed a program, funded by George Soros's Open Society and other groups, to show community organizers how to integrate voter registration into whatever they're doing, whether it's enrolling people for healthcare, public housing, or food stamps.

There's nothing wrong with encouraging voting. But a government employee is legally barred from saying you should become a Democrat. A community organizer can say it and will.

Covered California, that state's exchange, shows how helping the uninsured is being exploited for partisan purposes.

California lawmakers passed a law (Senate Bill 35) requiring that voter registration be part of the health insurance exchange.[26] Then in the spring of 2013, Covered California announced $37 million in grants to forty-eight organizations to build public awareness and prepare for the launch of Obamacare on October 1, 2013.[27]

Of the forty-eight organizations that got grants, only a handful were health-related. The California NAACP received $600,000 to do door-to-door canvassing and presentations at community organizations. Service Employees International Union received two grants totaling $2 million to make phone calls, robocalls, and go door to door.

Community Health Councils, a California organization with a long history of political activism against fracking, state budget cuts, and oil exploration, got $1 million to conduct presentations at community meetings and one-to-one sessions.[28] These organizations, closely allied with the Democratic Party, are being funded with your tax dollars to do "outreach," meaning the kind of phone banking and neighborhood solicitation that activists do to turn out the vote.

In addition, California's actual enrollment process is also outsourced to employees of community organizations, unions, and health clinics. After the first year, these assisters and navigators will be paid out of the revenues collected by the exchange. That means out of the premiums you pay.

This pattern is repeated in every state. Obamacare provides a steady stream of funding to the get-out-the-vote allies of the Democratic Party. The assisters will also guide the uninsured to sign up for whatever non-health social services they may be eligible for, including welfare, food stamps, and housing assistance, according to the navigators' manual prepared by the Community Health Councils for California's implementation.

Anyone familiar with the days of James Curley, Boss Tweed, and Tammany Hall gets the picture. If you were poor or a newcomer to this country, you went to the local ward boss and got whatever you needed in exchange for your vote.

The difference is that back then, politics was local. Now the Obama health law is institutionalizing this corrupt style of politics across the country. From New York to California, community activists and unions will be recruiting people to enroll in Obamacare and sign up to be part of the permanent, beholden Democratic voting majority.

CHAPTER FOUR

WHAT EMPLOYERS AND EMPLOYEES NEED TO KNOW

Facts You Need to Know:

- One-third of employers are considering dropping coverage because of Obamacare
- The federal government predicts the employer mandate will *reduce, rather than increase,* the number of people who get coverage at work
- Employers are barred from rewarding top managers or most-valued employees with more generous coverage

Most Americans get their health insurance through a job—their own, their spouse's, or a parent's. Employers voluntarily offer insurance in order to attract the best workforce and do the right thing.

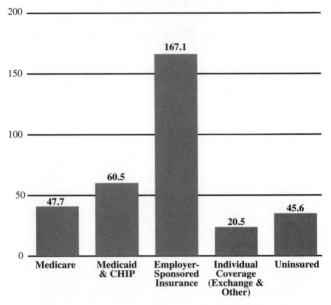

Health Insurance in America in 2011, before Obamacare's Full Implementation (in Millions)

Source: CMS, National Health Expenditure Projections 2012–2022, Table 17, at http://www.cms.gov /Research-Statistics-Data-and-Systems/Statistics-Trends-and-Reports/NationalHealthExpendData/ Downloads/Proj2012.pdf.

But if you have insurance at work, you may lose it soon. According to McKinsey & Company, a management consulting firm that did a broad survey shortly after Obamacare was enacted, one-third of employers are already considering dropping coverage for employees and their families. McKinsey found that among employers who have actually studied the law, the figure is even higher.[1]

That doesn't mean you will be uninsured. You won't have that choice. The IRS will require you to have insurance and attach proof of it when you file your federal income taxes. If your employer drops coverage in 2014, you will have to find an insurance broker, buy a plan on a state insurance exchange, or downgrade to Medicaid if you qualify.

A Mandate That Is Predicted to Reduce Coverage

One of the major goals of Obamacare is to increase the number of people with health insurance. But the employer mandate, which you'll learn more about in this chapter, could make employers unwilling to offer insurance. Even the federal government—the nonpartisan Congressional Budget Office—forecasts that fewer people will get coverage on the job after the employer mandate goes into effect than if Obamacare had not passed.[2]

Only the "Washington knows best" crowd could concoct a health law that makes it harder for you to keep your health plan—and your job.

The mandate requiring employers with fifty or more full-time workers to provide coverage is a major part of the Affordable Care Act. The law said it "shall" take effect beginning January 1, 2014. Then, ever so quietly, a low-level bureaucrat in the Obama administration slipped into the Treasury Notes blog (not exactly the *New York Times*) the big news that the mandate would be delayed for a full year—until January 1, 2015.

The president has no legal authority to change the law without Congress, but he quietly did it. The presidential edict took businesses, not-for-profits, even local governments and school districts by surprise. All had been preparing to comply with the mandate as of January 1, 2014. When you're running a business or an organization, nothing is worse than uncertainty and unpredictability. But that's what we're facing.

This chapter will tell you about the many requirements the law imposes on employers, in addition to the notorious mandate. It will also predict what's likely to happen to the mandate.

You don't need a crystal ball to see that the employer mandate may never be implemented. Yet most businesses have to prepare for it because it may be—and it's the law. Whether you run a business or simply get your own coverage through a job, you need to know the facts.

If You Get Your Insurance at Work, It Has Already Changed

You remember the president's promise, "If you like your health care plan, you'll be able to keep your health care plan, period."[3] That wasn't true. Regulations imposed by the Obama administration in June 2010, just weeks after the law was enacted, have compelled most employers to alter the coverage you get. The Obama regulators said at the time that up to 64 percent of large companies and 80 percent of small companies would be forced to give up what they offered at the time and make changes.[4] The regulations made coverage more expensive for employers, who generally pass that cost on to workers. Some employers—including for-profit companies and city governments—dropped coverage for spouses or part-time employees or asked employees to contribute more.

For example, United Parcel Service (UPS) announced in August 2013 that it would stop covering spouses who are eligible for coverage at their own job.[5] Home Depot dropped coverage for 20,000 part-timers.[6]

The costliest of these early Obamacare regulations were the ones keeping adult children up to age twenty-six on their parents' plans, and phasing out annual and lifetime limits on what medical expenses will be paid if you get sick. These are popular changes. But companies had to find ways to offset the costs. That was the point of a blunt letter Delta Air Lines' CEO sent to President Obama in June 2013.

The letter reminded the president that the goodies in Obamacare were hammering Delta's bottom line, hurting its ability to hire more people and to keep the company growing. Delta said that adding 8,000 adult children to its coverage cost the company $14 million a year.[7]

Illegal Waivers

As soon as those early Obamacare regulations were imposed, some companies and unions protested. They made it clear: exempt us from these rules or we will drop coverage for our workforce.

McDonald's warned that it would stop covering nearly 30,000 hourly restaurant workers. While many restaurants don't offer any coverage for hourly employees, McDonald's was providing mini-med plans—plans that cost very little ($14 a week for $2,000 coverage and $32 a week for $10,000 annual coverage). The philosophy behind these plans was that some coverage was better than none.

One of the early Obamacare regulations—requiring that 80 percent of premiums be spent on medical care—was a non-starter for mini-meds. Their administrative costs are far too high.[8] Other fast food companies and retailers that offered mini-meds also protested.

The protests worked. Nothing in the law empowered the Obama administration to exempt anyone, but the Secretary of Health and Human Services handed out 1,472 waivers to exempt certain companies and unions from the early provisions of Obamacare.[9]

The Employer Mandate

Will certain companies and unions also be granted waivers from the employer mandate? Nothing in the wording of the legislation gives the Obama administration authority to do that. Then again, the letter of the law didn't deter him from issuing the mini-med waivers—or postponing the employer mandate entirely for a year.

Here are the facts about Section 1513 of the Obama health law—called "Employer Responsibility."

The employer mandate requires that employers with fifty or more full-time workers must provide health coverage or pay a penalty. And not just any coverage, but a package of expensive benefits that the administration deems "essential."

In most states, the mandate will add $1.79 per hour to the cost of a full-time employee, and in New York and New Jersey (where health plans are more expensive), it will add a whopping $2 an hour or more, according to economist James Sherk of The Heritage Foundation.[10] This is the biggest government-imposed labor cost hike in American history.

Even employers who currently offer coverage voluntarily will be clobbered. They lose leeway about what benefits to offer and how much to ask workers to contribute. Your employer may very well decide that paying the $2,000-per-employee annual fine is cheaper and easier than complying with the mandate.

The devil is in the details:

1. Employers can no longer reward top managers or most-valued employees with fancier health insurance. The same plan must be offered to all employees for the sake of equality.

2. Once the mandate goes into effect, employers who don't provide coverage will be fined if an employee applies for Medicaid or a subsidy on the Obamacare exchange. The employer's fine will be calculated on the total number of employees minus thirty. So a business with fifty workers that doesn't provide insurance will be fined $2,000 x (50–30) = $40,000. If the business employs a hundred people instead of fifty, the fine will be $140,000. In calculating the fine, it doesn't matter how many employees apply for taxpayer subsidies or Medicaid. The fine is triggered once one employee applies.

3. To provide insurance that is "affordable," employers cannot ask workers to contribute more than 9.5 percent of their gross income. If the contribution exceeds that and an employee goes to the exchange for a

subsidized plan instead, the employer gets fined $3,000.

4. No one knows why the law discriminates against businesses with fifty or more employees. But it does. A fast food chain with forty-nine uninsured employees could be hit with a $40,000 fine for adding that fiftieth worker (50–30 = 20 x $2,000). Dan Danner, president and CEO of the National Federation of Independent Businesses, explained "the law's employer mandate effectively tells small businesses, 'Do not hire more than 49 employees.'"[11]

5. Employers who opt not to provide the mandated coverage will see their labor costs go up about 98 cents an hour. That's the $2,000 fine spread out over the 2,200 hours the average employee works. That's compared to the $1.79 an hour to provide the government-mandated plan.

6. Employers must offer family plans as well, but do not have to pay any portion of the cost of insuring spouses or dependents, according to an IRS clarification of the law's murky language. The bottom line is that some workers who now get family coverage

may get only individual coverage when and if the mandate goes into effect. Oops! That's exactly the opposite of what the president promised. Family coverage, under Obamacare, is expensive. It could add as much as $5 per hour to the cost of hiring a waitress or sales clerk, according to The Heritage Foundation.[12]

7. At the same time, Obamacare bars dependents from receiving exchange subsidies if a member of the family gets employer-provided "affordable" coverage. That has health advocates outraged.

8. Large groups and self-insured groups have slightly more leeway about what their coverage must include than small group employers (fewer than a hundred workers). Employers with small group plans must provide the ten essential health benefits listed in section 1302 of the law.

9. An astounding 61 percent of employees who get insurance at work are in self-insured plans.[13] Companies that self-insure pay their workers' medical bills directly, rather than paying premiums to a commercial insurer. It used to be that just very large

multi-state companies took this route. It spared them from numerous state insurance mandates and laws. But now even medium and small employers are doing it. One reason is that it protects them from several of Obamacare's rules, such as the 40 percent "Cadillac" tax punishing generous health coverage.

10. If you're in a self-insured plan, be aware that the "health reformers" are trying to make it harder for your employer to self-insure. From the "Washington knows best" point of view, self-insured employers are escaping government controls. Stay tuned for changes ahead.

Will Your Employer Drop Your Health Coverage?

If the mandate goes into effect, many employers will do simple arithmetic to answer that question. Here's the calculation:

EITHER provide a long list of essential benefits *and* pay taxes and fees levied on each covered employee *and* cope with numerous federal reporting requirements

OR

pay a $2,000-per-worker fine.

Some employers will conclude the fine is a bargain.

Deloitte Consulting estimates that nearly 10 percent of employers will drop coverage.[14] Lockton Benefit Group reports that 19 percent of their mid-size business clients are planning on dropping coverage, while the McKinsey survey of employers who already know what the new law says reports that 50 percent or more are planning to stop offering insurance.[15]

The Urban Institute argues that employers will still offer coverage to compete for the best workers, but in the current job market that argument is unconvincing.[16] Employers won't balk at providing the expensive mandated health plan to a $500,000-a-year heart surgeon or $250,000-a-year stockbroker. But the mandate could price a young unskilled job seeker out of the market.

If you work as a waitress, receptionist, sales clerk, or fast food chef, or in another modest-paying job, you may have to say good-bye to health insurance—and just hope your job doesn't disappear as well. Chili's Grill and Bar chain, which has almost 1,300 restaurants nationwide, is looking to eliminate busboys when the new health law goes into effect.[17]

Employers can't offset the new health insurance cost by cutting pay for minimum wage workers. There is no place to cut; the law won't allow it. Employers are left with these options:

1. Don't offer insurance and pay the fines.
2. Replace full-time workers with part-time workers.
3. Replace workers with automated teller machines and check-outs.

Part-Time Nation

So here's what we can expect if the employer mandate goes into effect. Look for more part-time jobs ahead. Noted economist, Robert J. Samuelson calls Obamacare a "job killer." He writes, "There's a powerful incentive to avoid Obamacare, either by not hiring or by pushing full-time workers under the 30-hour cap."[18]

In fact, the period from January 1, 2013, to July 31, 2013—when employers still expected the mandate to go into effect in 2014—produced a historic first: the shortest average work week on record, according to Labor Department data.[19] Employers were preparing to comply with the mandate. And a "look back period" in the law meant their legal obligations in 2014 would be calculated based on what they did in 2013. So in the first half of 2013, before the president delayed the mandate, employers aggressively reduced their full-time work-force and hired only part-timers for less than thirty hours a week.

Amazingly, during that period, 77 percent of the jobs created were part time. Fewer than one of four people hired got full-time work—the opposite of a normal economy. Job seekers were increasingly being offered twenty-nine hours or less.[20]

The Obamacare mandate was fast turning us into a nation of part-timers.

Americans were being forced to cobble together a living with two or three part-time jobs, if they could get them. An *Investor's Business Daily* analysis of Bureau of Labor Statistics data showed that the people hardest hit were nonsupervisory workers making $14.50 or less an hour in bakeries, home healthcare jobs, general merchandise retailers, and jobs in other low-paying industries.[21] Even organizations synonymous with "doing good"—such as the Salvation Army and Goodwill Industries—were cutting workers' hours.[22]

Not surprisingly, full-time job creation bounced back and part-time employment subsided as soon as the president delayed the employer mandate. The August 2013 employment data showed the stunning change.

Andrew Puzder, the CEO of CKE Restaurants, which operates Hardee's, told the *Wall Street Journal* that "the evidence that ObamaCare is having a negative impact on hiring is unequivocal, abundant, and consistent with common sense."[23]

Several members of Congress are pushing for legislation that would redefine a full-time employee as forty hours a week for the purposes of this law.

Redefine! That's what it always was until Obamacare came along.

Mid-Size Companies Are Hit the Hardest

Mid-size companies with slim profit margins will be affected most by the mandate. Grady Payne came to Washington, D.C., to warn the politicians how the added cost of health insurance will drive him out of business. Payne's company makes wooden crates at eleven plants in Texas, Oklahoma, Mississippi, Tennessee, Georgia, Florida, South Carolina, and Virginia.

Only about half of his employees currently get insurance at work because the other half don't feel that contributing to health insurance is a good way for them to spend their pay. But under the Obama health law, he will have to enroll them and set the employee contribution at a level deemed "affordable." He says it will be an "administrative nightmare."

His other option is to stop insuring his workers and pay the $2,000-per-worker fine, which will amount to $1 million a year. That's more than the company's annual profit. Payne told the politicians that his company is caught in "no-man's land" between the small businesses that don't have to provide insurance and the big companies and unions that somehow manage to get waivers.[24]

The delay of the employer mandate came as good news for Grady Payne. He said, "I'd like to see it repealed."[25]

Will the Employer Mandate Ever Be Enforced?

On July 3, 2013, shortly after the Obama administration leaked out the news that the employer mandate would not go into effect on January 1, 2014, White House advisor Valerie Jarrett depicted the change as a mere "tweaking." Some tweaking. It affected roughly 10 million workers plus their dependents.

Looking back, the delay seemed to be part of a string of desperate attempts by the administration to prop up the health exchanges, which were scheduled to open three months later.

Weeks before the employer mandate ploy, Secretary of Health and Human Services Kathleen Sebelius had implored the NBA and the NFL to sell young fans on the idea of buying coverage on the exchanges. Young healthy enrollees are needed to offset the costs of the sick and middle-aged and prevent premiums from spiking even higher than they were already expected to go. But the sports leagues said no to shilling for Obamacare.

That's when the administration postponed the employer mandate—making sacrificial lambs of the 6.9 million uninsured full-time workers whose employers otherwise would have been compelled to start providing them with coverage on January 1, 2014, or pay a fine.[26]

Add another 3.1 million workers covered by mini-med plans. The waivers allowing these plans were to expire on January 1, 2014, leaving these workers uninsured as well.

All in all, 10 million workers were affected. Delaying the employer mandate but not the individual mandate meant that these workers and their dependents would have to sign up on the exchanges or pay a tax for being uninsured. Voilà! Delaying the mandate instantly increased the likelihood of more healthy exchange enrollees.

It's plausible that the administration will continue to delay the employer mandate as part of its broader campaign to move people into the exchanges and Medicaid, under the thumb of government. Never mind the increasing burden this puts on taxpayers.

From the beginning of the campaign to pass the Affordable Care Act, its supporters insisted it would liberate people from dependence on employer-provided insurance. That makes no sense if there's an employer mandate in the law.

In October 2013, four months after the president delayed the employer mandate, House Minority Leader Nancy Pelosi, California Democrat, hailed the launch of the rest of Obamacare as meaning "the freedom to pursue your happiness. Whether you want to be a writer, a cameraman, to be self-employed, start your own business, change jobs, whatever you wanted to do" without losing your health coverage.[27] That doesn't sound like a Democratic Party committed to the employer mandate. Mandating that employers provide coverage made it easier to push the Affordable Care Act through Congress—it made the law appear to be paid for—but that mandate may never be implemented.

CHAPTER FIVE

PAYING FOR MORE BENEFITS YOU DON'T WANT

Facts You Need to Know:

- "Free" preventive care is not free. You pay for it up front in your premium
- The Obamacare law expands the services insurers *must* cover and you *must* pay for. That will raise your premium
- Covering children up to age twenty-six on their parent's plan raises *your* premium even if you don't have adult children

There is no tooth fairy. The more your health plan covers and pays for, the more it's going to cost. Obamacare imposes an expensive array of new mandates on the insurance industry. That means, ultimately, it's imposing higher premiums on you.

"Free Preventive Care"

Section 2713 of the law, which went into effect in September 2010, prohibits co-pays for preventive services.

The president has boasted that the new health law provides "free" preventive care, but it's not free. It's pre-paid. The law forces you to pay for a mammogram, a Pap smear, and a colonoscopy up front, when you pay your premium—whether you intend to get the tests or not. If you do get the test, there will be no deductible or co-pay. But clearly the test isn't free.

Being forced to pay up front for a colonoscopy feels almost as bad as having to get one.

There are several other provisions, called "consumer protections" in the law, which are already driving up premiums.

No Annual or Lifetime Caps on Benefits

As of September 2010, insurance companies can no longer put a lifetime cap on what they will pay out to cover your medical costs. This requirement applies even to the small number of "grandfathered plans" that survive under Obamacare.

The new law also phases out annual caps on payouts. Annual caps were raised to at least $2 million in September 2012 and eliminated in January 2014.

It sounds wonderful, but it also means you can no longer have the option of being covered by one of those mini-med plans commonly offered to entry-level workers in many industries.

In fact, no sooner was this new provision put into effect than the White House was inundated with complaints from some of the biggest employers in America. They said that they couldn't afford to provide comprehensive insurance for low-wage hourly workers.

The White House responded by granting a total of 1,472 waivers to certain companies and unions, exempting them from the law. But in 2014 those waivers run out. If you currently have a mini-med plan at work, be aware that you're likely to lose coverage.

Children Can Be Insured on Their Parent's Plan to Age Twenty-Six

This is another whopper of a premium hiker. Many parents and their adult children like this idea, and the provision could have gotten through Congress with or without Obamacare. The provision took effect September 2010, and it applies to adult children. (But parents on Medicare and certain retirement plans cannot add their adult children.) Previously, coverage for dependent children ended at nineteen, or a few years later for full-time students. Of course, this new provision benefits some families at the expense of others. If you don't have adult children, you are paying a higher premium for your family plan to keep your neighbor's adult child covered.

More Premium Hikes to Come

But the biggest premium hikes are ahead. Even before Congress passed Obamacare, the Congressional Budget Office warned that individual and small group premiums would be higher under the law than if the law had not been passed. In other words, members of Congress voted for Obamacare knowing it would raise your insurance costs. A major reason is the one-size-fits-all benefit package.

The "essential benefits" provision means that every health plan sold to you on the exchanges or provided through an employer will have to be packed with benefits—all costing something—in order for it to meet the legal requirement that you have "qualified" health insurance. You have to pay for inpatient substance abuse treatment coverage even if you have no intention of ever taking drugs, for example.

It's like passing a law that the only car you can buy is a fully loaded Cadillac.

This is the provision that led to the avalanche of cancellations starting in the fall of 2013.

No Rejections for Pre-Existing Conditions

No other feature of the Obama health law has gotten more attention than the provision that goes into effect in 2014 prohibiting insurance companies from denying coverage to people with pre-existing conditions. Often this is the one-liner used to justify the entire 2,572-page law.

People with hypertension, diabetes, and other pre-existing conditions should be able to get health insurance. But the fact is, most already can.

Less than one percent of the U.S. population has been denied coverage for a pre-existing condition, according to federal Health and Human Services data.[1] Even before Obamacare, no one with a pre-existing condition could be barred from employer-provided coverage (the way most people are insured), or from Medicare and Medicaid.

Denials came only in the small individual market (serving just 5 percent of the population). Even there, four out of five people with pre-existing conditions had no difficulty getting coverage, according to HHS data.

Pre-existing conditions simply do not constitute a major problem, in terms of the numbers of people affected. But you know the drill for politicians. Create a crisis and then purport to solve it.

The Obama healthcare law set up a temporary federal high-risk pool for applicants with pre-existing conditions.

It has been a flop. Only 105,000 people with medical conditions gained coverage, according to National Conference of State Legislatures data.[2] That's 105,000 out of a population of over 300 million—less than 0.035 percent of the people in the United States. Hardly enough to justify overhauling the healthcare system. Surely there must be some less costly way—less costly not just in dollars spent, but also in deleterious effects on our healthcare system and on millions of Americans' health—to meet the genuine needs of this tiny minority?

In most states, people with pre-existing conditions are already getting help through a subsidized high-risk pool. That's the right approach, and far better than what New York and New Jersey have done. These two states require insurers to sell policies to healthy people and sick people at the same price. The result is the highest premiums in the country, because healthy people drop out to avoid paying the high premiums—which of course, pushes premiums even higher.

Obamacare follows the New York/New Jersey approach but makes buying insurance mandatory. How many young healthy people will go along with that, rather than forking over the penalty? Economists disagree. The jury is still out.

CHAPTER SIX

MEDICAID NATION

Facts You Need to Know:

- Expanding Medicaid is the chief way that the law covers the previously uninsured
- Surgery patients with Medicaid face a higher risk of dying than patients with no insurance at all
- Expanding Medicaid raises premiums for people with private insurance

Expanding Medicaid is the key component of Obamacare. Even after the June 2012 United States Supreme Court ruling giving states the option of *not* expanding Medicaid, this expansion is still the way most previously uninsured people gain coverage. The new law transforms Medicaid from a temporary safety net to a permanent entitlement in place of private insurance.

All states have Medicaid, though some give it a distinctive name, such as TennCare in Tennessee and Medi-Cal in California. Medicaid was created in 1965, and CHIP (the Children's Health Insurance Program) was added to it in 1997. Ever since 1965 the federal government has set minimum standards but otherwise given states leeway to determine eligibility and benefits based on what state taxpayers wanted and state budgets could handle. Federal taxpayers paid half the cost in some states and a bit more in others. Even so, Medicaid has become the biggest item in many states' budgets and the second biggest in the rest.

Fast forward to 2014. The Obama health law urges states to open up Medicaid to many more people and pledges to pay all or nearly all the cost (90 to 100 percent) for those newly eligible.

New Medicaid Rules in Some States

States that went along with the new federal rules opened up Medicaid to residents with incomes up to 133 percent of the poverty level (roughly $33,000 for a family of four in 2014). States adopting the federal rules also opened Medicaid to childless adults, not just pregnant women and families, and disregarded an applicant's assets when determining eligibility. People with limited incomes are eligible, no matter how much money they have in the bank or what else they may own.[1]

These changes alone were predicted to cause a 57 percent increase in Medicaid enrollment in Texas, a 49 percent increase in Oklahoma, a 42 percent increase in Florida, a 41 percent increase in Virginia, and similarly huge enrollment increases in nearly a dozen other states.[2] For that reason several governors, including Texas governor Rick Perry, announced that their states will not go along with the Medicaid expansion.

25 States and the District of Columbia Have Expanded Medicaid

States that have expanded Medicaid as of November 10, 2013

States that have not expanded Medicaid as of November 10, 2013

If You're a Taxpayer

As of November 1, 2013, twenty-five states and the District of Columbia had decided to go along with the expansion, looking at the federal promise of funding as a pot of gold. But a report of the nonpartisan State Budget Crisis Task Force, released July 17, 2012, and chaired by two big-time Democrats—former lieutenant governor of New York Richard Ravitch and former Federal Reserve chairman Paul Volcker—warned that Medicaid expansion could push states into financial crisis if the federal government breaks its promise to fully fund it. That could be a punishing blow to anyone who pays state taxes.

Will the federal government go back on its word? It wouldn't be the first time government broke a promise. Though the Obama health law says the federal government will pay the tab for expanding Medicaid, any future Congress can undo that commitment. If that happens, state taxpayers will be left holding the bag, just when state budgets (and taxpayers) are already strained to the breaking point. Governor Mike Pence of Indiana said the federal promise is "the classic gift of a baby elephant," with the government only promising to pay for hay the first few years.[3]

Of course whether it's the states paying or the federal government paying, it's really YOU the taxpayer paying. Under the Obama health law, Medicaid becomes the fastest-growing part of the nation's healthcare spending, outpacing Medicare—despite the aging of the baby boomers.

If You Lose Coverage at Work and Wind Up on Medicaid

In addition to newly eligibles, an unknown number of low-income workers who have private insurance are expected to lose it and be dumped into Medicaid, according to government actuaries. If you are a waitress, sales clerk, or entry-level job holder, that could be you. I use the term "dumped" because seldom do people with private health insurance volunteer to switch to Medicaid. But when the new mandates on employers start in 2015, many businesses will say that covering employees with the "Washington knows best" mandates is too expensive, and stop doing it. Your boss could be one of them. If you're in a relatively low-paying job, your next stop may be Medicaid.

Healthcare advocates are already warning of the unintended consequences of the huge increase in Medicaid enrollment for truly poor Americans. It's already very difficult to find doctors willing to take Medicaid. The dean and CEO of Johns Hopkins Medicine, Edward Miller, warned that the expansion of Medicaid enrollment could have "catastrophic effects" at places like Hopkins.[4]

Sadly, Medicaid care is often inferior care. University of Virginia researchers reviewed the experiences of nearly 900,000 patients undergoing eight different surgical procedures. Shockingly they found that Medicaid patients were 50 percent more likely to die in the hospital after surgery than patients with private coverage. Even more amazing, according to the *Annals of Internal Medicine*, Medicaid patients were 13 percent more likely to die than patients with no insurance at all.[5] Researchers also found that Medicaid patients who undergo angioplasty to open up clogged arteries are twice as apt to have another heart attack or other serious circulatory problems as patients with private insurance.[6]

What the research shows is that Medicaid patients get worse care—but, ironically, not cheaper care. The inferior care they get results in more complications, and the complications lead to longer hospital stays and higher costs. It's only reasonable to question whether expanding Medicaid is a good idea when patients already on Medicaid are getting dangerous care at high costs.

Heart patients on Medicaid are less likely to receive angioplasty when they need it, and asthmatic children on Medicaid don't see specialists. In fact, few specialists in any field take Medicaid.[7] When people with heart disease on Medicaid can't see a cardiologist, expanding the Medicaid program and worsening the shortage of specialists could be deadly. No wonder health advocates are concerned.

Medicaid Shortchanges Doctors, Patients, and Taxpayers

If you're likely to be on Medicaid, these are important issues to know about. The fact is, most doctors either don't take Medicaid or limit how many Medicaid patients they will see because Medicaid shortchanges them.

Medicaid pays on average about 86 cents to 91 cents for every $1 of care delivered. It shortchanges hospitals and doctors. To make ends meet, doctors and hospitals have to charge privately insured patients more. That pushes up your premium. The well known healthcare consultancy Milliman & Robertson estimates that shortchanging by government programs forces families with private insurance to pay at least $1,500 a year more in added premiums. That's *before* the new Medicaid expansion. These experts caution that once Obamacare's vast Medicaid expansion occurs, private premiums will be pushed even higher.[8]

The Obama health law offers only a band-aid solution. It increases what Medicaid pays primary care doctors—but only for a year!

The Medicaid Expansion Will Push Up Private Premiums

The more Medicaid is expanded, the higher private premiums will go. As a taxpayer, you pay for Medicaid three times—first when you pay your federal taxes, then when you pay your state taxes, and a third time when you pay your own insurance bill.

So get ready for higher tax bills and long waits for Medicaid patients to be treated as Medicaid rolls explode in many states. When Obamacare's health exchanges officially launched on October 1, only a trickle of people enrolled in the plans that require you to pay. But the Medicaid numbers shot up immediately. In Washington state, 87 percent of the people who enrolled the first three weeks were signing up for Medicaid. It's free for the enrollee, though not for taxpayers.[9]

Maryland, California, and Washington are using aggressive tactics to get people who already use food stamps and other public assistance to sign up for Medicaid, according to Matt Salo, executive director of the National Association of Medicaid Directors. The states are also signing up residents of homeless shelters and inmates being discharged from prison.[10]

The higher Medicaid enrollment goes, the higher private premiums will go, too. Private premiums are estimated by the Medicare actuaries to rise an astounding 7.1 percent in 2014, the year the mandated benefits and Medicaid expansion go into effect.[11]

No matter what else the Affordable Care Act does, it is pushing the U.S. closer to being a Medicaid nation. Politically left-wing people who favor government-run "single payer" healthcare applaud Medicaid as a national model. But the substandard care, government controls, and long waits for doctors make Medicaid more of a national disgrace than a national model.

CHAPTER SEVEN

OBAMACARE RAIDS MEDICARE AND HURTS SENIORS

Facts You Need to Know:

- The Obama health law awards bonus points to hospitals that spend the least on seniors
- Hospitals will be whacked with demerits for care that seniors consume up to thirty days after leaving the hospital, including physical therapy
- In October 2013, Medicare Advantage plans started dropping physicians, particularly specialists, from their networks in response to cuts from Washington

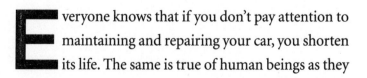 veryone knows that if you don't pay attention to maintaining and repairing your car, you shorten its life. The same is true of human beings as they

age. We need medical care to avoid becoming clunkers—worn out, parked in wheelchairs or nursing homes.

For nearly half a century, Medicare has enabled seniors to get that care. But the Obama health law removes over half a trillion dollars in future funding from Medicare over the next decade. The new law:

- Slashes what doctors, hospitals, homecare agencies, hospice care, and dialysis centers are paid to care for the elderly,
- Penalizes hospitals for providing generous care, and
- Cuts support from Medicare Advantage plans

These cuts are being made just when 30 percent more people will be entering Medicare, as baby boomers turn sixty-five. The numbers do not add up. Baby boomers who are counting on Medicare will get less care than seniors currently get. Data from the Obama administration's own actuaries indicate that Medicare will spend $1,431 less per senior in 2019 than if the law hadn't passed.[1]

Paying for the New Entitlements, 2013–22: Seniors Pay the Lion's Share

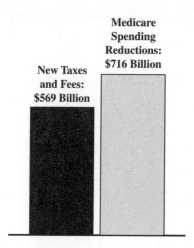

The Congressional Budget Office has estimated that the revenue from Obamacare's new taxes, fees, and other provisions will be $569 billion from 2013 to 2022. Meanwhile, the CBO estimated that Obamacare would reduce spending on Medicare by $716 billion over the same time period.

Source: Congressional Budget Office, letter to Hon. John Boehner, July 24, 2012, http://www.cbo.gov/publication/43471.

Across-the-Board Payment Cuts

Doctors, hospitals, hospice care, nursing homes, and dialysis centers will be paid substantially less to care for seniors than if the law had not been passed, and in some cases even less than Medicaid pays. The Obama administration's own former Chief Actuary of Medicare, Richard

S. Foster, bravely warned Congress that the cuts would reduce seniors' ability to get the care they need.[2]

Foster warned that unless these cuts are repealed, about 15 percent of hospitals could stop accepting Medicare. Where will seniors go if their local hospital stops taking Medicare?

Other hospitals will be forced to operate in an environment of scarcity, with as many as 40 percent in the red, according to Foster. That will mean fewer nurses on the floor, fewer cleaners, and longer waits for high-tech diagnostic tests. These cutbacks will affect all patients.

Obamacare's defenders say that cutting Medicare payments to hospitals will knock out waste and excessive profits. Untrue. Medicare already pays hospitals less than the actual cost of caring for a senior, on average 91 cents for every dollar of care. No profit there. Pushing down the reimbursement rate further, as the Obama health law does, will force hospitals to spread nurses thinner. When Medicare reduced payment rates to hospitals as part of the Balanced Budget Act of 1997, hospitals incurring the largest cuts laid off nurses. Eventually patients at these hospitals had a 6 to 8 percent worse chance of surviving a heart attack and going home, according to a National Bureau of Economic Research report.[3]

Peter Orszag, former Budget Director and Obamacare supporter, ignores this evidence and tries to reassure

seniors that Medicare spending could be cut by 30 percent without harming seniors.[4] He cites the *Dartmouth
Atlas of Health Care 2008*, which tries to prove that
patients who get less care—fewer hospital days, doctors
visits, and imaging tests—have the same medical "outcomes" as patients who get more care.[5] But read the fine
print.

The Dartmouth authors arrived at their dubious conclusion by studying the records of patients who had
already died. Of course the patients treated at the high-
spending hospitals and the low-spending hospitals had
the same end result. They were all dead!

Fortunately, researchers have set the record straight.
Data published in the *Archives of Internal Medicine* show
that seniors treated in hospitals providing more intense
care and greater spending have a better chance of recover-
ing, going home, and resuming their lives.[6] Seniors treated
at the lowest-spending hospitals die needlessly. Researchers found that 13,815 California seniors treated at low-
spending hospitals would have survived and left the hospital had they received the extra care provided at higher-
spending hospitals. Reducing care at the very end of life
may be wise, but these across-the-board Medicare cuts
will result in reduced care for all patients, including those
who could survive their illnesses and go home if they get
the care they need.

New Medicare Efficiency Measures

In addition to the across-the-board cuts in payments to hospitals, Section 3000 of the Obama health law actually awards bonus points to the hospitals that spend *the least* per elderly patient. The bonus system went into effect on October 1, 2012. Hospitals that spend the least "per Medicare beneficiary" get rewarded, and hospitals that spend more get whacked with demerits. This is despite evidence that patients have a better chance of surviving at higher-spending hospitals. Hospitals will even be penalized for care consumed up to thirty days after patients are discharged—for example, for outpatient physical therapy following a hip or knee replacement.

Subjecting Seniors to the Ravages of Aging

Five procedures have virtually transformed the experience of aging for Americans: knee replacements, hip replacements, angioplasty, bypass surgery, and cataract operations. Older people used to languish in nursing homes or be trapped in wheelchairs. Now many can continue to lead active lives. The Obama health law threatens to undo that progress. The across-the-board cuts in hospital payments and the rewards for hospitals that spend the least per senior will make all these procedures harder to get and less safe.

Astoundingly, doctors who treat seniors will be paid only about a third as much as doctors treating privately insured patients, according to former Chief Actuary Foster. On July 13, 2011, he warned Congress that seniors will have difficulty finding a doctor to treat them. Even doctors who do continue to take Medicare won't want to spend time doing procedures such as knee replacements when the pay is so low. Yet the law bars them from providing the care their patients need for an extra fee. You're trapped.

Some people seem to think too many seniors are getting these procedures. At a town hall debate in 2009, President Obama told a woman, "Maybe you're better off not having the surgery, but taking the painkiller."[7]

Science proves that attitude is wrong. Knee replacements, for example, not only relieve pain but also save lives. Seniors with severe osteoarthritis who opt for a knee replacement are less apt to succumb to heart failure and have a 50 percent higher chance of being alive five years later than arthritic seniors who don't undergo the procedure, according to *Journal of the American Medical Association* research.[8]

When assessing what the impact of Medicare cuts will be on you and your family, ignore the political rhetoric and look at the scientific evidence. The cuts will doom seniors to more painful aging and shorter lives.

Dr. Seymour Cohen, an oncologist named to "America's Top Doctors," summarized the dire consequences during a physicians' forum on the health law: "When we went to medical school, people used to die at 66, 67, and 68. Medicare paid for two or three years. Social Security paid for two or three years. We're the bad guys. We're responsible for keeping people alive to 85. So we're now going to try to change health care because people are living too long. It just doesn't make very good sense to me."[9]

Prevention

Section 4104(a) of the new law expressly authorizes the Secretary of Health and Human Services to reduce preventive services for seniors based on the recommendations of the U.S. Preventive Services Task Force. (That's the panel that recently caused public outrage by saying women ages forty to forty-nine and older than seventy-four should no longer get routine annual mammograms.) A half-page later, the law empowers the Secretary to "increase" preventive services for Medicaid recipients. The winners and losers here could not be clearer.

The law says,

> SEC. 4105(a). Evidence-Based Coverage of Pre-ventative Services in Medicare. (n) Authority to Modify or Eliminate Coverage of Certain Preventative Services.—Notwithstanding any other provision of this title, effective beginning on January 1, 2010, if the Secretary determines appropriate, the Secretary may—
>
> (I) modify—
>
> (A) the coverage of any preventative service described in subparagraph (A) of section 1861 (ddd)(3) to the extent that such modification is consistent with the recommendations of the United States Preventative Service Task Force...

Advantage Plans

Nearly one out of every four seniors is in a private Medi-care Advantage plan, rather than traditional Medicare.

Medicare Advantage was launched in 2003 to give seniors the option of choosing a private health plan with the government paying most of the cost. These plans cost the government (and thus taxpayers) about 10 percent more, but they also provide seniors with more benefits.

They are hugely popular because of extras such as vision and dental care—and occasionally even gym memberships—that traditional Medicare doesn't cover.

Medicare Advantage is singled out for big funding cuts under the Obama health law. Medicare Advantage funding will be slashed by 27 percent—meaning $3,700 less per year for each senior enrolled by 2017. The result is that plans will offer fewer extras, and may drop the doctors you currently use.

In October 2013 UnitedHealthcare cut many Florida doctors and hospitals from its AARP plan network there, including Tampa Eye Institute, Moffit Cancer Center, and St. Luke's Cataract & Laser Institute. The insurer ran a full-page ad in local papers explaining that "severe funding reductions for Medicare Advantage plans that have come from Washington" are behind the change.[10]

UnitedHealthcare New England dropped dozens of doctors from its network at the same time. Steven Detoy, a spokesman for the Rhode Island Medical Society, explained that these doctors were not dropped from the insurer's commercial plans, only from the plan for seniors. Evidently these doctors, mostly specialists, see patients who are seriously ill, and therefore expensive to treat.[11]

Emblem Health in New York State sent letters to seniors telling them their doctors were being dropped because of Obamacare. Lung cancer patient Jeannette Campregon, seventy-nine, received a letter saying her internist was terminated from her plan. "I'm going absolutely nuts," said Campregon. "I don't want to change my doctor."[12]

Medicare actuaries predict that enrollment in Medicare Advantage will plummet to half what it would be without Obamacare.[13] The president promised, "If you like your health care plan, you'll be able to keep your health care plan, period."[14] That's definitely not true for the 7.4 million seniors expected to lose the choice of Medicare Advantage.

The Independent Payment Advisory Board

Over and above the half trillion in cuts to future Medicare funding, Section 3405 of the Obama health law creates a fifteen-member board of unelected cost-cutters called the Independent Payment Advisory Board (IPAB). It's meant to be "independent" of the public and shielded from the wrath of senior voters.

The IPAB's job is to identify further cuts in what doctors, hospitals, hospice care, and other providers are paid to care for seniors. IPAB can't cut benefits, we're told. But those are weasel words. IPAB can push the payment for a hip replacement lower and lower, until it is so low that medical professionals can no longer afford to provide that treatment. Even the Congressional Budget Office has warned that as the nation's debt crisis worsens, Medicare benefits will be put on the IPAB chopping block.

Even Howard Dean, a former chairman of the Democratic National Committee, attacked IPAB as "essentially a health-care rationing body.... the IPAB will be able to stop certain treatments its members do not favor by simply setting rates to levels where no doctor or hospital will perform them."[15] IPAB is a radical departure from Medicare as we've known it. In creating IPAB, Congress cedes nearly all control over Medicare spending to unelected bureaucrats. Congress is admitting it doesn't want to make unpopular cuts and then face seniors. The Obama health law says that whatever cuts IPAB "recommends" automatically go into effect *unless* Congress enacts a different set of Medicare changes with the same net savings. That arrangement—making IPAB into a lawmaking body— turns the U.S. Constitution on its head, many argue.

Already IPAB has aroused opposition all across the political spectrum, even from supporters of the Obama health law, such as former Representative Pete Stark (California Democrat) and the AARP. Perhaps anticipating the opposition, the law's drafters included a provision laughable in its brazen defiance of the U.S. Constitution.

This provision states that IPAB can be repealed only in a tiny window of time. The repeal must be submitted to Congress between January 1 and February 1, 2017 (not sooner or later) and enacted by August 15 of that year. In reality, no Congress can bind any future Congress. IPAB can be repealed any time the people's elected representatives choose to repeal it, and many will say the sooner the better.

Raiding Medicare, Not Saving It

You've probably heard the claim that the cuts in future Medicare spending will secure the program's financial future. That claim is even repeated in Medicare's mailings to seniors. But the truth is, Medicare is being raided, not saved. The funds taken from Medicare are not set aside to extend the program's solvency. Instead they are spent on new entitlements for people under sixty-five. Former Chief Actuary of Medicare Richard Foster and Director of the Congressional Budget Office Douglas Elmendorf candidly told Congress that Medicare cuts would not prolong the life of the program. To claim otherwise would be cooking the books.[16]

Closing the Donut Hole: "Let Them Eat Cake"

Politicians have talked much less about the cuts to future Medicare funding than about the sweeteners. The most publicized is "closing the donut hole," which means gradually adding Medicare Part D drug coverage for seniors who use between $2,800 and $6,400 worth of prescriptions a year.

Previously, Medicare Part D paid for most medication expenses up to the $2,800 mark, but then seniors who needed more drugs had to pay 100 percent of the cost until their purchases reached a whopping $6,400 a year. For the small number of seniors with costly chronic illnesses, the donut hole was a big problem. The new law gradually fills in this coverage gap with money provided partly by the federal government (taxpayers) and partly by rebates sent directly to consumers by pharmaceutical companies. If you've ever fallen into the donut hole, your Medicare Part D drug plan will tell you how to get help in the future.

But don't be misled. The cuts in Medicare funding are ten times as large as the sweeteners.[17]

CHAPTER EIGHT

THE TAX MAN COMETH

Facts You Need to Know:

- Your ability to deduct medical expenses was reduced starting in 2013
- Your tax-free contributions to a Flexible Savings Account were also limited starting in 2013
- Generous "Cadillac" health plans will be taxed at 40 percent starting in 2018

There is no question that seniors bear the biggest cost of Obamacare. But taxpayers also pay for it. There are twenty new taxes or tax hikes in the law. It's "the largest set of tax law changes in twenty years," according to Treasury Inspector General J. Russell George.[1] The IRS says it will need more than a thousand new auditors and $359 million in 2012 alone to administer the new health law.[2]

Medicare and Payroll Tax Hikes, Plus New Taxes on Tanning Salons and Home Sales

One of the biggest sources of new tax revenue will be a hike in the Medicare hospital insurance tax—though the extra revenue will *not* be going to Medicare. Currently, the tax amounts to 2.9 percent of your gross pay, with employer and employee each paying in 1.45 percent. The new law raises the employee portion to 2.35 percent for high earners (with no hike in the employer contribution). Individuals who earn more than $200,000 a year and couples who make more than $250,000 per year are considered high earners; they pay the higher rate starting in 2013.

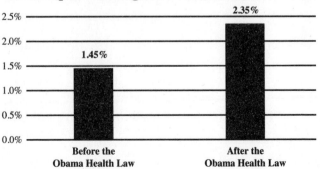

Increased Medicare Hospital Insurance Tax (2013 & After) for Couples Earning More than $250,000 a Year

The even bigger change is a new 3.8 percent Medicare tax on "unearned income," meaning gains from stocks, bonds, dividends, rents, vacation homes, and even, under some circumstances, the sale of your primary residence. (Once again, the name is misleading because the revenue will not go to Medicare.) A person with modest income could become a "high earner" and be hit with that 3.8 percent tax if he sells his home and makes a large profit. This tax applies *in addition to capital gains taxes*. Note: people who sell their primary residence get a once-in-a-lifetime $500,000 exclusion.

**New Medicare Investment
Income Tax (2013 & After)
for Couples Earning More than $250,000 a Year**

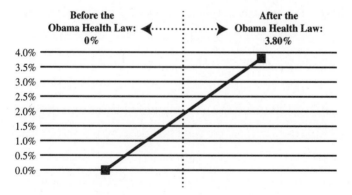

Obamacare also imposes a new 10 percent tax on indoor tanning services, which must be paid either by the tanning salon or the customer. This new tax is expected to raise about $1.5 billion in revenue over the next decade.[3]

New Taxes on Pharmaceuticals, Medical Devices, and Health Insurance Companies

Even if you're neither a high earner nor a tanning salon customer, you'll be affected by the new Obama taxes. Several taxes, totaling an estimated $107 billion over the law's first decade, will technically hit insurers, medical device companies, and pharmaceutical companies, but you can assume the costs will be passed on to you, the consumer, in the form of higher prices.

The new health law slaps a tax on all health insurers, based on the number of premiums they collect. This tax will hit small businesses, their employees, and people who pay for their own individual policies. One of the goals of health reform was to make coverage more affordable. But this tax will do just the opposite. The Joint Committee and the CBO confirm that this tax will be passed on to consumers and raise their premiums, costing the average family $300 to $400 a year in added premium costs. A troubling 87 percent of small business owners will be hurt by this tax.[4] Unlike big companies that self-insure, small business owners buy policies for their workforce and will ultimately pay this premium tax.

Other taxes nominally on the healthcare industry include a tax on the manufacture or importation of medical devices, which will likely raise the cost of hip and knee replacements, and taxes on brand name pharmaceuticals.

Aside from the indirect impact of these taxes on the industry, other changes in the tax rules may affect you.

Higher Penalty on Health Savings Accounts Disbursements

Do you have a Health Savings Account? The new law doubles the IRS penalty from 10 percent to 20 percent for non-allowable purchases made using funds in Health Savings Accounts or Flexible Savings Accounts.

Starting in 2011, funds in these accounts may be used only to buy prescription drugs, not over-the-counter drugs. If you want to buy Tylenol or Advil with these funds, you'll need to get a prescription first.

New Limits on FSAs

Do you have a Flexible Savings Account? Beginning in 2013, employees will be able to make tax-free contributions of only $2,500 a year, down from the unlimited amount in the past. Overall, the new law is stacked against you paying for your healthcare out of pocket or on your own, rather than with insurance.

Fewer Medical Deductions

Do you usually deduct medical expenses when you do your taxes? Up to now, you could deduct expenses that exceeded 7.5 percent of your income. Beginning in 2013, you'll lose the medical expenses deduction unless your expenses exceed 10 percent of your income. (For seniors, however, the change comes in 2017, not 2013.)

Penalties against Employers and Individuals

Another revenue source is what employers and individuals will be forced to pay if they are caught without government-prescribed health insurance. By 2022, the CBO estimates that these penalties will amount to $172 billion.[5]

Excise Tax on "Cadillac" Health Insurance

Finally, beginning in 2018, a "Cadillac" tax on health plans that cost more than $10,200 for an individual or $27,500 for a family is scheduled to go into effect.[6] The tax is a whopping 40 percent, imposed on the insurer who sells the plan—but of course, it will be passed on to the consumer. It is a major source of payment for the

Obamacare entitlements, providing $111 billion by 2022—the second biggest revenue producer among the twenty new taxes in the law.

Despite the tax's nickname, "Cadillac" health plans are held by a much broader range of people than Wall Street tycoons and other "one percenters." Many union workers have them. In fact, the tax was originally supposed to take effect much sooner, but powerful unions pushed Congress to both delay its effect and exclude many union workers in "high-risk" occupations. Longshoremen even got the law amended after it was passed, to expressly identify their occupation as high risk and immune from the tax.

So will the Cadillac tax ever take effect? It's impossible to say. It's hard to imagine that a future president and Congress will have more fortitude than the law's namesake has to impose it.

Obamacare and the Deficit

Defenders of the Obama health law cite claims by the Congressional Budget Office that repealing the health law would increase the deficit. Repeal would cancel $890 billion in new entitlements, said the CBO, but also eliminate revenues of greater magnitude.[7]

Don't be bamboozled by the CBO's budgetary gymnastics. Just because Obamacare—in theory—raises more money than it spends is hardly reason to keep it, or any law.

The Obama health law creates two costly giveaways—an expansion of Medicaid and subsidies for private health plan purchasers—and pays for them by hiking taxes and raiding funds previously designated for Medicare. The tax hikes and reductions in funds to care for the elderly (each over half a trillion dollars) together total more than the entitlements during the next ten years, says the CBO, and produce a small $109 billion surplus. Repealing the law would erase that tiny surplus. So what! Repeal would reduce government spending, lower taxes, and undo the evisceration of Medicare: all good things.

Recently published projections from the Centers for Medicare & Medicaid Services (CMS) fill in the grim picture of what Obamacare will do to the nation, and correct dangerous misconceptions voiced by some of the nation's top politicians who responded to the CBO report.

Senate Majority Leader Harry Reid, Nevada Democrat, has said the CBO report "confirms what we've been saying all along: the Affordable Care Act saves lots of money."[8] Untrue. CMS data show cumulative health spending over the next decade will be $621 billion higher than if the law had not been passed.[9] Healthcare spending as a share of gross domestic product will rise from 17.9 percent in 2010 to 19.9 percent in 2022, and government (and ultimately the taxpayers) will be paying for a larger share of it than ever before.[10]

House Democratic Whip Steny Hoyer of Maryland has said that the CBO "makes it very clear: the Affordable Care Act is controlling the growth of healthcare costs."[11] Also untrue. Healthcare spending was growing at the slowest rate in many decades when Obamacare was passed, inching up only 3.9 percent in 2009 and again in 2010. But CMS predicts spending will shoot up 6.1 percent in 2014, when Obamacare goes into full effect.[12]

In worse news, private insurance premiums will increase 7.1 percent that year, says CMS, which is 4.1 percentage points higher than if the health law had not been passed.

The only area of healthcare spending that will grow more slowly is Medicare, because of the cuts made by Obamacare and further cuts under the Budget Control Act of 2011. Seniors are bearing the brunt in every budget deal made by the Obama administration.

Don't be misled by the CBO's fuzzy math and Washington's infatuation with deficit reduction. In Washington today, "deficit reduction" is code for increasing taxes faster than spending. It means freedom reduction. If we're really interested in cutting the deficit, we need entitlement reform to reduce spending. And the best way to start is by repealing the two new entitlements in the Obama health law before they go into effect.

CHAPTER NINE

DOCTORS REJECT OBAMACARE

Facts You Need to Know:

- A 2013 Deloitte national survey of 47,000 doctors found that fewer than one-third had decided to accept health exchange insurance
- The Obama health law gives the Secretary of Health and Human Services power over doctors' decisions, even for patients with private health plans they paid for themselves
- Many doctors are considering leaving the medical profession because of Obamacare

Aside from seniors, the group most opposed to the Obama health law is doctors. Of course, they want their patients to have access to affordable healthcare—the nominal purpose of the law.

But many doctors oppose the law because it will drown them in red tape and paperwork, reduce their earnings, and empower government bureaucrats to interfere in how they care for patients.

The American Medical Association

Physician opposition to the Affordable Care Act undoubtedly surprises many people because the American Medical Association (AMA) endorsed the law. But only about 17 percent of practicing doctors belonged to the AMA at the time, and AMA membership dropped in 2010 and 2011 because of the organization's support for Obamacare.[1] Doctors see Obamacare as a threat to their livelihood—and their patients' health.

"Doctors Going Broke"

"Doctors Going Broke" was a CNN headline on January 5, 2012.[2] Stingy payments from government programs such as Medicare and Medicaid are largely to blame. On average, Medicare pays only 81 percent of what a private insurer pays for the same care.

Medicaid rates are even worse, on average only 56 percent of what private insurers pay.[3] The new health law clobbers physicians' livelihoods in three ways—by vastly expanding Medicaid enrollments, severely cutting payment rates for patients on Medicare, and crowding out private insurance with the exchanges.

The new health exchanges don't treat doctors any more fairly than the government entitlements. To keep sky-high premiums on the exchanges from spiking even higher, insurance companies are paying hospitals and doctors far less than they are paid to see patients with other types of private plans. Health exchange plans are, in that sense, similar to Medicaid. For example, most health plans on the California exchange don't permit patients to be treated at Cedars-Sinai in Los Angeles or the University of California hospitals. In New York City, New York Presbyterian, another top-drawer medical system, is excluded from most exchange plans.

A poll conducted by the Medical Society of the State of New York in October 2013 found that only 23 percent of doctors had decided to participate in exchange plans.

There's more to physician discontent than just dollars and cents, however. Doctors are "drowning in Alphabet Soup," as Dr. Hal Scherz puts it. Scherz is founder and president of Docs4PatientCare, a nationwide physicians group that opposes Obamacare. He calls the Obama health law a "compliance nightmare," and cites the huge number of reporting requirements that will turn doctors into paper pushers instead of healers.[4]

Beginning in 2015, doctors who don't submit a long list of health measurements on their patients will be penalized by losing 1.5 percent of their Medicare reimbursements—a serious matter since Medicare already shortchanges physicians. Measuring quality is important, but who is going to do all the paperwork?

Worse than these hurdles of paperwork and inadequate payment rates, what doctors object to most is the government's interference in how they care for patients. When Medicare and Medicaid were established nearly a half-century ago, the law said that the federal government could not interfere with treatment decisions. Over the decades, some of that protection was whittled away. Now the Obama health law puts government directly in charge.

Controlling Medical Decisions

In fact, the framework for top-down control over the practice of medicine was actually slipped into the "stimulus" legislation, or American Recovery and Reinvestment Act, passed in February 2009. One provision called for doctors and hospitals to install and use electronic health information technology. Beginning in 2014, Medicare and other federal programs will impose financial penalties on doctors and hospitals that are not "meaningful users" of the technology.

What is "meaningful use"? Electronic health records can help make sure that if you're injured and rushed to the emergency room, your records—including, for example, the information that you are allergic to penicillin—will reach the hospital ahead of you, even if you are thousands of miles from home. This technology has the potential to save lives and money. Unfortunately, "meaningful use" means a lot more than that. Doctors already see the signs that the technology will put "Washington knows best" bureaucrats in charge at the bedside—using computers to tell doctors what to do.

Dr. David Blumenthal, the first appointee to head President Obama's Office of the National Coordinator for Health Information Technology, said at the outset that his job was not about "just putting machinery in offices." It's about control. Blumenthal predicted "many physicians and hospitals may rebel—petitioning Congress to change the law or just resigning themselves to…penalties."[5] Dr. Hayward K. Kwerling, an internal medicine physician in Massachusetts, blasted the Obama administration for "placing the politicians in the middle of the exam room."[6]

How much leeway will doctors have to order the tests and treatments they think are needed? It's hard to say, because the stimulus legislation empowered the government to make the standard of "meaningful use" more "stringent" over time.

The Obama health law extends control of doctors beyond what they do for patients in government programs. For the first time in history, this law empowers the federal government to dictate how doctors treat privately insured patients—patients who aren't on Medicaid or Medicare but instead have private insurance from companies such as Aetna or Cigna. Even if you pay your own premium, the government is still in charge. For many healthcare advocates as well as physicians, this is the most important issue of all: the transfer of decision-making authority from the doctor at your bedside to the federal government.

Section 1311(h)(1) of the Obama health law states that you have to be in a "qualified plan," and qualified plans can pay only doctors who follow the dictates of the federal government. The new law says that the Secretary of Health and Human Services—appointed by the president—can impose any regulation to "improve health care quality." That can literally cover *everything in medicine*, from whether you get a hip replacement to what tests your doctor orders to follow up on equivocal mammogram results.

For some doctors and patients, the answer is to escape to concierge medicine. Patients pay an annual fee (as much as $500 to $3,000 per year) to sign up with a primary care physician. In return, patients get more time from their doctor, faster appointments, and freedom from government dictates. As Dr. Bradley Allen, a pediatric heart surgeon and former professor at the Children's Heart Institute in Houston, explained, "Doctors and patients who can afford it love concierge medicine. It allows treatment to be administered as the doctor sees fit, instead of as if the patient is on an assembly line with care directed on orders from Washington."[7] The controls on doctors embedded in the Obama health law have made some physicians pessimistic about the future of their profession and even disheartened enough to quit practicing. Americans are already facing a doctor shortage. The profession's gloomy assessment of the new law's impact on their finances, their job satisfaction, and the future quality of medicine will likely worsen that shortage.

Deloitte's 2013 survey of physician opinion found that three-quarters think the best and brightest may not consider a career in medicine.[8]

CHAPTER TEN

OBAMACARE VS.
THE RULE OF LAW

Facts You Need to Know:

- There are many legal challenges to Obamacare ahead—it's a full-employment project for lawyers
- The Supreme Court has ruled twice in modern times that presidents cannot repeal, delay, or change parts of a law without Congress
- The Supreme Court ruled in 2006 that the federal government must not "define general standards of medical practice in every locality." That's precisely what the Obama health law does

Just minutes after President Obama signed the Patient Protection and Affordable Care Act into law on March 23, 2010, the state of Florida filed a lawsuit challenging its constitutionality. Virginia also sued, challenging the mandate. All in all, twenty-eight states have challenged Obamacare. On June 28, 2012, the high court ruled that Congress can compel Americans to buy insurance. That ruling opened the way for implementation of nearly every aspect of the law.

But there is more courtroom drama ahead. Americans of every political persuasion, from far left to far right, are challenging specific provisions of the law, or how President Obama has changed the law. At stake is the survival of the rule of law, the principle that keeps Americans free.

Expanding Executive Power

President Obama has been unrelenting in his attempts to expand executive power—his power—beyond what the Constitution allows. The president has dispensed with large sections of the Affordable Care Act.

These illegal changes to the law are not victimless crimes. Suspending the employer mandate shifts costs from employers to taxpayers. Suspending the cap on out-of-pocket expenses helps insurers (and keeps premiums from spiking even higher) but punishes the seriously ill who were initial supporters of the law. Advocacy groups such as the American Cancer Society have expressed concern at this sudden change. And the subsidy for members of Congress and their staff will set taxpayers back $55 million a year.

But the biggest loser is the rule of law.

In the future, there will be many demands made to change or delay parts of Obamacare. The critical issue is who will make changes to the law. Allowing the president to continue to pick and choose what parts of the law are enforced is a threat to our freedom.

The Employer Mandate

Consider the employer mandate, originally a linchpin of the law and then mysteriously gone. What happened there reveals the administration's ploys to patch up an unworkable law, disregarding how millions of Americans get clobbered by the unpredictable, lawless changes.

The law requires that employers with fifty or more full-time workers provide coverage or pay a penalty. On July 2, 2013, the administration said that it won't enforce the employer mandate until 2015, though the Affordable Care Act states that it "shall" be in effect as of January 1, 2014. That delay appeared to be a desperate strategy to prop up the health exchanges.

Three days after the employer mandate suspension, on July 5, 2013, came another whopper. The administration revealed that it would skip the health law's requirement that applicants seeking taxpayer subsidies to pay for their insurance have their income and insurance eligibility verified. This was another ploy to open the enrollment floodgates to get people into the exchanges. Too bad again for taxpayers.

Rule by Edict

At an August 9, 2013, press conference, the president was asked where he gets the authority to delay the employer mandate. Obama said that "in a normal political environment, it would have been easier for me to simply call up the speaker and say, you know what, this is a tweak that doesn't go to the essence of the law.... let's make a technical change to the law. That would be the normal thing that I would prefer to do."

But, Obama explained, he took a different route because Republicans control the House of Representatives and ardently oppose Obamacare. As he has so often done, Obama indicated that when Congress won't agree with what he wants, he will act alone. That should send shivers through freedom-loving Americans.

Obama's stance reveals how disconnected he is from this nation's history and constitutional principles—amazing for someone who claims to be a constitutional expert. Divided government is the norm in the United States.

Most modern presidents have had to govern with an uncooperative Congress or at least one house of Congress controlled by the other major party.

With the exception of Richard Nixon, these presidents—from Eisenhower to Reagan to Clinton and both Bushes—have not tried to exempt themselves from the Constitution.

Obama is different. Three days after his inauguration in 2009, President Obama silenced Republican lawmakers who voiced concern about the enormous spending in his stimulus bill by uttering two brash words: "I won."[1]

That was his governing philosophy as he rammed through the American Recovery and Reinvestment Act in 2009. Remember "shovel ready"? But in the fall of 2010, Republicans swept into control of the House of Representatives and since then, Obama's agenda has been stalled.

With little prospect of gaining control of the House in 2014, Obama resorted to disregarding the Constitution's limits on presidential power rather than bargain with congressional Republicans.

Obama insisted that his presidential authority was enough to suspend the employer mandate, even when Republicans were willing to make the delay legal by enacting the Authority for Mandate Delay Act. Lawmakers in both parties were uncomfortable with Obama's edict. Democratic Senator Tom Harkin of Iowa, an Obama ally, questioned whether the president had the authority to delay the mandate. "This was the law," Harkin said. "How can they change the law?"[2] On July 17, the House passed the bill to legalize the delay, with thirteen Democrats adding their support. Obama threatened to veto the legislation if it made it through the Senate and onto his desk, insisting that it was unnecessary.

Unnecessary? Only if the office of president has lawmaking powers. It does not.

The United States Supreme Court has ruled twice in modern times that presidents cannot delay, repeal, or change parts of the law.[3]

But going to court to thwart a power-hungry president is slow and costly. The Constitution's framers provided a more practical way: withholding funds.

It's checks and balances in action. Madison declared in *The Federalist* No. 58 that Congress' authority over spending would be the "most complete and effectual tool" to stop a president from grabbing more power than the Constitution allows.

Senator Lee's Stand for the Constitution

On July 17, 2013, Senator Mike Lee, Republican of Utah, took a page out of Madison's playbook. Lee urged

Congress to vote against any continuing resolution to fund the federal government after September 30 as long as it funded Obamacare. Lee made the president's illegal changes to the healthcare law the centerpiece of his defunding effort: "Laws are supposed to be made by Congress, not…the president, who has now amended Obamacare twice. Once in saying, individuals have to comply with the law during their first year but employers don't. Then in saying, we aren't even going to require people to prove their income."[4]

Lee said that if the administration was not prepared to fully enforce the Affordable Care Act as enacted, it should agree to delay the entire law and remove the funding from the budget.

Lee's constitutional case was airtight. Unfortunately, it was drowned out by accusations that he and his supporters were "arsonists," "obstructionists," and radicals. The three major networks never covered the unconstitutionality of the president lifting the employer mandate by fiat. And even leading Republicans who went along with defunding failed to articulate it as a constitutional battle. Speaker of the House John Boehner instead attacked the president for favoring big business and giving them a delay he was unwilling to give individuals.

Before long, even Republican Senators who had stood with Lee lost their nerve, worried about the political repercussions of a government shutdown on their own reelection chances. Republican Senator Richard Burr of North Carolina called Lee's defunding approach "the dumbest idea I've ever heard."[5]

There's nothing dumb about protecting the Constitution. Members of Congress took an oath to defend it. If not now, when?

Don't hold your breath waiting for Congress to uphold the rule of law. Contrary to Madison's hopes, relief may come faster in the courts.

On October 1, 2013, Judicial Watch filed a lawsuit in federal court on behalf of a Florida orthodontist who had expended thousands of dollars in legal fees preparing for the employer mandate, only to see his money wasted and his business plans bungled when the administration suddenly dispensed with it. The lawsuit, filed in the U.S. District Court for the Southern District of Florida, argues that the U.S. Treasury Department (responsible for enforcing the mandate) violated the Administrative Procedures Act, which forbids federal agencies from replacing statutory authority with their own discretion. Thomas Fitton, president of Judicial Watch, explained that "under the U.S. Constitution, the law can only be changed by legislation passed by Congress and signed by the president."[6]

When Senator Mike Lee made that argument, he was shouted down in the court of public opinion. But things look more promising in federal court.

On October 22, 2013, U.S. District Judge Paul Friedman denied the Obama administration's request to dismiss another lawsuit challenging its "rewrite the law" strategy. The Affordable Care Act says people who enroll in plans offered on exchanges "established by the states" are eligible for premium subsidies depending on their household income. Only fourteen states established exchanges. The other thirty-six states declined, letting the federal government do it. To weasel a way around that unexpected snafu, the IRS ignored the letter of the law and pushed ahead to provide subsidies in all fifty states.

The Obama administration also lost its bid to dismiss a lawsuit brought by Oklahoma's Attorney General Scott Pruitt on the same issue. Pruitt told the court the federal government can't rewrite the law. The Obama administration told the judge there was no merit to the case, but U.S. District Judge Ronald White disagreed and let Pruitt's case proceed.

The president brushes off questions about his selective enforcement of the law as mere partisan attacks, but federal judges obviously don't see it that way. And it's not just about healthcare. Take a look at this ruling on another matter entirely, the president's determination to implement his own energy policy, no matter what Congress has enacted. The Obama administration's bruising defeat in the D.C. Circuit Court of Appeals on August 13, 2013, suggests he may lose these healthcare lawsuits as well. The court ruled that the Obama administration, including Energy Secretary Stephen Chu, could not ignore a 2002 statute requiring certification of Yucca Mountain as a nuclear waste site.

Judge Brett Kavanaugh ruled that "our constitutional system of separation of powers would be significantly altered, if we were to allow executive and independent agencies to disregard federal law.... Under Article II of the Constitution and relevant Supreme Court precedents, the President must follow statutory mandates so long as there is appropriated money available and the President has no constitutional objection to the statute."[7]

That ruling smashes the president's strategy of delaying, patching, and rewriting parts of the Affordable Care Act—including setting aside the employer mandate and allowing subsidies in states that did not establish exchanges—to create the illusion that the law is workable.

When Judicial Watch president Tom Fitton announced its lawsuit against the president's constant changes to the law, he paraphrased Ulysses S. Grant: "The best way to ensure the repeal of a bad law is to enforce it vigorously."[8] Let the public feel the brunt of Obamacare.

And they will, if these lawsuits challenging the subsidies in thirty-six states succeed. People there will still be legally required to have insurance, but they will have to pay sticker-shock premiums without any subsidy. Obamacare premiums are on average twice as high for men than if the law had not passed, according to the Manhattan Institute, with whopping deductibles of $5,000 for the Bronze Plan and $3,000 for Silver. A defeat for the administration would also mean employers are shielded from penalties for failing to insure workers. Those penalties are triggered when an employee receives a subsidy on an exchange—another example of the mind-numbing complexity of the interconnected morass that is the Affordable Care Act.

Preserving the Rule of Law

"The Supreme Court ruled it constitutional," Obama often says about his signature law, the Affordable Care Act. But dozens of lawsuits challenging the administration's footloose implementation are making their way through the courts.

Still, courts alone cannot ensure the survival of our republic. We the people must elect vigilant lawmakers committed to defending the Constitution, and hold them accountable when they don't. Members of Congress take an oath to uphold the Constitution, but most need a refresher course. Many put party loyalty ahead of fidelity to the Constitution. Nothing better illustrates that than the corrupt way the Affordable Care Act was passed, in violation of the origination clause, with barely a murmur of protest over that issue.

> Article 1, Section 7 of the U.S. Constitution states: "All Bills for raising Revenue shall originate in the House of Representatives; but the Senate may propose or concur with Amendments as on other Bills."

All bills to raise revenue are supposed to originate in the House of Representatives. But as Michael Patrick Leahy notes in his book *Covenant of Liberty,*

On September 17, 2009, Congressman Charlie Rangel introduced a bill in the House, H.R. 3590, the "Service Members Home Ownership Tax Act of 2009," whose purpose was "to amend the Internal Revenue Code of 1986 to modify the first-time homebuyers credit in the case of members of the Armed Forces and certain other Federal employees." The bill passed the House on October 8 by a 416–0 vote.

On November 19, Harry Reid introduced his own version of H.R. 3590 in the Senate. He took the bill that had been unanimously passed by the House, renamed it the "Patient Protection and Affordable Care Act," deleted all its contents after the first sentence, and replaced it with totally different content. What followed was the first pass of the Senate version of ObamaCare.[9]

As public outrage grows over high premiums, cancelled health plans, and job cutbacks, the polls will reflect it, and the phones in those congressional offices will be ringing off the hook with complaining constituents demanding immediate solutions.

That's when lawmakers need to look to the Constitution to be their guide. Don't go to the president like supplicants, asking him to delay deadlines and waive penalties that are clearly spelled out in the Affordable Care Act. And if the president proposes some quick fix, don't accede to it. It's up to Congress, not the president, to change the law. The president's job is to faithfully execute it.

In these months of controversy over the health law, there is more at stake than healthcare. This president is threatening the rule of law, the bedrock of our freedom.

The more times Obama is permitted to trample the Constitution, the more freedom we've lost. Madison's warning in *The Federalist* No. 48 still applies: "An elective despotism is not the government we fought for."[10]

Can the Federal Government Standardize Medical Care?

Can the federal government dictate how doctors treat privately insured patients? In all likelihood, this provision (Section 1311(h) of the law) will be challenged before the pro-privacy high court.

Consider how the court ruled in *Gonzalez v. Oregon* (2006). Oregon had passed a Death with Dignity Act allowing lethal drugs to terminally ill patients who requested them. The Bush administration argued that assisted suicide was not "legitimate" medical care, and therefore federal agents could halt the use of the drugs under federal drug enforcement laws. The Supreme Court ruled 6–3 against the Bush administration's interference. Such intrusion, the Court said, would "effect a radical shift of authority from the States to the Federal Government to define general standards of medical practice in every locality."[11] That's exactly what the Obama health law does.

Before the current Obamacare debate, the public dis-
cussed government interference in medical decisions
largely in one context: abortion. When a lower federal
court struck down the Partial Birth Abortion Ban Act in
2004 (a decision later reversed by the Supreme Court),
Planned Parenthood president Gloria Feldt said, "This
ruling is a critical step toward ensuring that women and
doctors—not politicians—can make private, personal
health care decisions."[12] During the litigation, federal
authorities requested access to medical records to determine whether partial-birth-abortion procedures were
ever medically necessary. Privacy advocates defeated every
request.

The Obama health law raises the same medical privacy
issues in a broader context than abortion. The mandate for
electronic medical records creates a "tell-all" relationship
with every doctor you see. See a psychiatrist? Your foot
doctor will know about it. So will many non-physicians
who have access to the data. The National Committee on
Vital and Health Statistics, a federal advisory committee,
proposed permitting patients to carve out categories of
information, such as mental or reproductive health, from
their records. The Goldwater Institute, a free market think
tank suing to overturn the law, argues that the law violates
privacy rights by compelling Americans to share "with
millions of strangers who are not physicians confidential
private and personal medical history information they do

not wish to share."[13] There is no doubt these privacy concerns will have their day in court.

The Independent
Payment Advisory Board

The Independent Payment Advisory Board is "independent in the worst sense of the word," Diane Cohen of the legal think tank the Goldwater Institute told Congress. IPAB is "independent of the will of the people."[14]

The Obama health law says that IPAB's czars "recommend" what doctors and institutions are paid. But that is slippery language. IPAB's recommendations automatically become law unless Congress passes—with a three-fifth's supermajority in the Senate—a medical spending plan achieving the same "savings."

These IPAB czars make laws affecting our healthcare unless Congress enacts legislation to accomplish the same end. The people's *elected* representatives are not even given the option of rejecting the Medicare cuts altogether and determining that cutting Medicare by that amount would be too severe and harmful.

The Supreme Court has not looked favorably on such exemptions from popular oversight. For example, in the high court's 2010 ruling in *Free Enterprise Fund v. Public Company Accounting Oversight Board*, the justices ruled that a board created to administer Sarbanes-Oxley had too much independence. The Constitution does not permit Congress, which has to face the people on election day, to delegate its responsibilities to unelected boards and councils.

Members of Congress swear to uphold the Constitution, but they routinely enact laws without giving the Constitution a moment's thought. Many are ignorant of what it says. They should be required to take a course.

CHAPTER ELEVEN

IF YOU LIKE YOUR GOD, YOU CAN KEEP YOUR GOD

Facts You Need to Know:

- Hospitals, religious colleges, charities, and even orders of nuns are waging legal battles against the president's birth control mandate
- Most of the for-profit companies challenging the president's birth control mandate are succeeding. As of November 1, 2013, the score was thirty-one court victories and only five defeats
- A federal judge has ruled that there are other ways for the government to provide contraception than requiring religious employers to pay for it

The First Amendment

The Bill of Rights makes protection of religion its first priority. Its framers put religion right at the top, in the First Amendment. Government is barred from "prohibiting the free exercise" of religion. But the Obama administration is testing that prohibition, requiring Christians to provide their employees with health plans that cover sterilization, birth control, and even "morning after" pills.

The Gilardi Brothers

On November 1, the Gilardi brothers, devout Roman Catholics who operate their own fresh produce business in Ohio, won round two in a First Amendment battle against the White House. The Obama administration tried to claim that freedom of religion means freedom to pray, not necessarily to practice your beliefs.[1] Once you leave church, you have to obey government regulations, even when they conflict with your faith.

Francis and Philip Gilardi insisted on living their beliefs as they run their business. For a decade, they've provided health insurance for their four hundred employees but excluded abortion drugs, contraception, and sterilization.[2] These conflict with Catholic teachings.

Nevertheless, the Obama administration requires all health plans to provide them. On January 2, 2013, the

Gilardi brothers sued in federal court, asking for temporary protection from the $14 million annual penalty they would face for not complying. A lower federal court turned down the Gilardi brothers, but the United States Court of Appeals for the District of Columbia later granted their request.

Judge Janice Rogers Brown ruled that if you like your God, you can keep your God. Your freedom to practice your faith isn't limited to praying or attending worship services. Quoting from the Bible, she reminded the government's lawyers, "Faith without works is dead."[3] If the Gilardi brothers want to paint signs on their trucks saying "It's not a choice, it's a child," and decline to provide contraception products to their employees, that's their right.[4]

Judge Brown cited a 1963 Supreme Court ruling by Chief Justice William Brennan that the government may not "penalize or discriminate against individuals because they hold religious views abhorrent to the authorities."[5]

The law appears to be on the Gilardis' side. The Religious Freedom Restoration Act of 1993 says a person can opt out of a law if obeying it would substantially diminish their fidelity to their religious principles.[6] There are exceptions, said Judge Brown, when the government has a compelling goal and no other way to achieve it. But Judge Brown made the commonsense observation that there are other ways to provide contraceptives to women who need them.

These products already are dispensed at federally funded community health clinics and at Planned Parenthood sites. Access does not depend on employer coverage. So why is the Obama administration doggedly waging this legal war?

More than three dozen for-profit companies owned by Catholics, Mennonites, and other people with religious scruples are in court resisting the administration's requirement. So far, six federal appeals courts have ruled on these cases, with four deciding for religious freedom, and two siding with the Obama administration.[7] Next stop is the Supreme Court.

Hobby Lobby

The Obama administration has requested the Court hear its case against David Green and his wife, who own Hobby Lobby craft stores and Mardel Christian bookstore. The Greens close their stores on Sundays and try to operate according to Biblical principles, which in their view means not providing the morning after pills known as Plan B and Ella to employees.[8]

When the Greens prevailed in lower federal court, the *Los Angeles Times* objected, saying, "A hobby shop is not a church."[9] The *New York Times* called the court's decision "a warped view" because "some employers can get out of complying with the new law...."[10]

Actually, nothing in the Affordable Care Act guarantees coverage for birth control. The Secretary of Health and Human Services—a presidential appointee—decides what your plan covers. President Obama and HHS Secretary Kathleen Sebelius said all plans must cover birth control. Future administrations can change that edict. Amazingly, women's rights groups have not objected to leaving this matter to the whim of whoever occupies the White House.

The dissenting judge in the Gilardi decision, Harry T. Edwards, argued that the Gilardis "cannot...invoke their personal religious values to deny employees the benefit of laws enacted to promote employee welfare."[11] But Edwards glossed over the fact that Congress didn't enact the contraceptive requirement. It's very unlikely such a divisive mandate could have passed Congress.

Blame the Obama administration for putting the mere convenience of birth control users ahead of Americans' freedom to practice what they preach.

Geneva College Wins an Injunction

On June 18, 2013, Geneva College won an injunction preventing the Obama administration from fining it for refusing to provide the government-mandated methods of birth control. Geneva College was the first non-profit religious institution to be granted an injunction, but over three dozen similar institutions have filed lawsuits seeking relief from the president's mandate.

Geneva College, founded in 1848, defines its mission as educating students to serve Christ. It was founded by the Reformed Presbyterian Church of North America.

The college has a proud history of civil disobedience against unjust laws. In the 1860s, it served as a station on the Underground Railroad to hide and transport escaped slaves. Today it is fighting against a government mandate it says unfairly discriminates against Christian institutions while offering waivers and exceptions to many unions and corporations, as well as some religious groups that oppose the concept of insurance.

The college's curriculum includes pro-life activities for students, alumni, and staff. And its health insurance coverage for employees and students bans artificial interference with the creation of life. Geneva College argues that its policy does not deny women access to contraceptives, because they are widely available outside the college.

Waging War against Nuns

Despite the rising number of litigants resisting the president's birth control mandate, he continues his high-stakes constitutional battle. Why is the president doubling down in his war against religious conviction?

On September 24, 2013, the Becket Fund for Religious Liberty filed a lawsuit on behalf of the Little Sisters of the Poor, an international Roman Catholic order that operates homes for needy elderly people in thirty-one countries. Sister Loraine Marie explained, "We cannot violate our vows by participating in the government's program to provide access to abortion inducing drugs." Little Sisters refuses to include these drugs in its employee health plans.

This is the first class action lawsuit against the mandate. The Little Sisters of the Poor was joined by hundreds of Catholic non-profit ministries.

The Obama administration narrowly defines "religious employer" to exclude organizations such as the Little Sisters, who serve non-Catholics as well as Catholics. Cardinal Timothy Dolan, Archbishop of New York, explains, "We don't serve people because they're Catholic; we serve them because we are, and it's a moral imperative for us to do so."[12]

"The Sisters should obviously be exempted as 'religious employers,' but the government has refused to expand its definition," said Mark Rienzi, Senior Counsel for the Becket Fund for Religious Liberty. "These women just want to take care of the elderly poor without being forced to violate the faith that animates their work. The money they collect should be used to care for the poor like it always has—and not to pay the IRS."[13]

The administration claims that the religious groups want to deny contraceptives to women. But the litigants point out how readily available contraceptives are, and argue that if the government can force religious institutions to violate their most deeply held beliefs, the government's power is without limit.

The Archdiocese of New York

The Archdiocese of New York is also suing to stop the president from imposing his birth control mandate on Catholic institutions. In court documents filed September 26, 2013, the Archdiocese declared what is at stake: "Before the Court is a question central to the country's centuries-old commitment to religious freedom: absent an interest of the highest order, can the government force religious organizations to take actions that violate their sincerely held religious beliefs?"[14] The lawsuit goes on to say that the Obamacare birth control mandate would force the New York Archdiocese "to facilitate conduct that is diametrically opposed to their religious beliefs."[15]

CHAPTER TWELVE

WASHINGTON'S MISGUIDED VIEWS ON HEALTH REFORM

Facts You Need to Know:

- Despite President Obama's frequent claims of "skyrocketing" costs, healthcare spending before Obamacare was passed was increasing more slowly than at any time in the last half-century
- The Obama health law is forcing premiums to go up
- Obamacare's emphasis on preventing sickness rather than treating it will shortchange the seriously ill

The 2,572-page Obama health law is packed with thousands of inscrutable passages. This guide is designed to decode them. But to make wise decisions about Obamacare, you also need to translate the claims made about healthcare by Washington politicians.

One misconception in particular can be dangerous to your wallet. Four others are dangerous to your health. Here they are, straight from the mouths of Washington experts and parroted day after day by the media.

1. "Skyrocketing costs" are making it impossible for families to afford health insurance. Without health reform, soaring health costs will destroy our economy. These doomsday warnings, which were instrumental in the passage of Obamacare, were simply untrue. At the time, healthcare spending was increasing more slowly than at any time in the last half-century. Spending increased 10.3 percent in 1970 and 13 percent in 1980, but only 3.9 percent in 2009 and 2010.

National Health Expenditure Annual Growth from Previous Year (1970–2014)

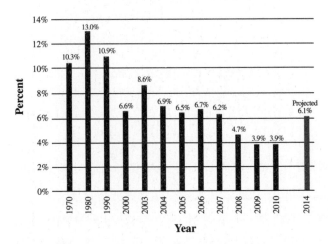

Source: CMS

Sadly the changes imposed by the new Obama health law will force up healthcare spending and premiums. The actuaries at the Centers for Medicare & Medicaid Services predict that spending will shoot up to 19.8 percent of GDP by 2020, up from 16.6 percent before the health law was passed.[1]

Premiums are already soaring and will continue to rise. Now that government requires you to buy a health plan packed full of government-mandated "essential benefits," it is going to cost more.

The Obama health law continues a pernicious trend, started in many states, to require health insurance plans to cover more and more. Since 1975, the share of healthcare Americans pay for out of their own pockets, rather than through insurance, has steadily declined, all the while causing premiums to rise *faster* than health costs.

Share of Personal Healthcare Expenditures Paid out of Pocket

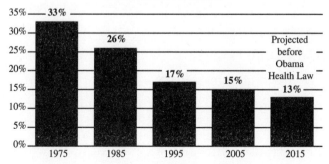

Out-of-Pocket Spending Declining Even before the Obama Health Law

Source: Congressional Budget Office

New York is a case study of bad insurance policy made by venal lawmakers in exchange for campaign contributions from lobbyists. Over the years, lobbyists for chiropractors, acupuncturists, mental health professionals, wig makers, and others rewarded the legislature for passing laws requiring that every health plan cover all these services—fifty-one requirements in all. Each mandate may add just half a percent to the cost of insurance, but that totals a 25 percent premium increase. As I've said before, it's like passing a law that the only car you can buy is a fully loaded Cadillac sedan.

There's a better way. New Jersey saw health plan enrollment dropping, so the state let insurers offer pared-down plans. Sales boomed. New Jersey, with half the population of New York, has three times as many privately insured residents, notes health policy expert Tarren Bragdon of the Empire Center for Policy Research.[2]

This lesson was lost on the "Washington knows best" experts. They repeated the exact mistake New York made, insisting on an expensive "comprehensive" health plan. That means no choices for consumers.

2. "We have to get to a system of keeping people well, rather than treating sickness," said the director of the White House Office of Health Reform, Nancy-Ann DeParle, on March 23, 2009.[3] That would make sense if all disease were behavior-related, but many cancers and other diseases are linked to genetics or unknown causes. DeParle's pronouncement echoes how Sir Michael Rawlins, a British health official, explained his nation's low cancer survival rate. The British National Health Service, he said, has to be fair to all patients, "not just the patients with macular degeneration or breast cancer or renal cancer. If we spend a lot of money on a few patients, we have less money to spend on everyone else. We are not trying to be unkind or cruel. We are trying to look after everybody."[4]

This approach—spreading the care thinly and widely—is deadly for those people with serious illness. In the U.S., about 5 percent of the populace needs 50 percent of the care according to the federal Agency for Healthcare Research and Quality.[5] Healthcare needs are very skewed. The drumbeat heard in Washington, D.C., to shift resources from treatment to prevention should worry any family dealing with Alzheimer's, Parkinson's, cerebral palsy, or a history of cancer.

3. The U.S. needs to slow the development and diffusion of new medical technology. Imagine any industry or nation thriving on such a philosophy. Yet that misconception is driving "reform" in Washington, D.C. Dr. Ezekiel Emanuel, one of the most influential advisors on the legislation, criticized Americans for being enamored with technology.[6]

New technology accounts for more spending increases than any other factor, even the aging of the population. But a 2008 report from the Congressional Budget Office reminded us that these innovations "permit the treatment of previously untreatable conditions."[7]

Walk into an electronics store, and you will see an array of products that didn't exist a year earlier. The same is true if you go into the hospital. Treatments for heart disease and strokes are as unlike care in the 1980s as flat-screen televisions are unlike the early black-and-white sets.

If you had a heart attack in the 1980s and made it to the hospital alive, you still had only a 60 percent chance of surviving until the end of the year. Now your chance is over 90 percent.[8]

Overall health spending could easily be reduced by settling for the standard of care and symptom relief available to patients in previous decades, warns the CBO. But there is no demand for 1980s medicine, even at 1980s prices, and in ten years no one will want 2014 medicine at today's prices, either.

4. "The only way to slow Medicare spending is to slow overall health system spending through comprehensive and carefully crafted legislation," declared Secretary of Health and Human Services Kathleen Sebelius.[9]

Forcing Americans to settle for a lower standard of medical care in order to save Medicare is like forcing all Americans to go on diets and buy fewer groceries because the food stamp program is running out of money.

Medicare can be fixed without putting the nation on a regimen of medical scarcity, with fewer nurses in the hospital, less access to technology, and pressures on doctors to do less. The safe alternative is to reduce the government's share of the cost of healthcare, rather than reducing the nation's overall standard of care. That can be accomplished by inching up the eligibility age for Medicare and asking wealthy seniors to pay more.

But the Obama health law moves the nation in the opposite direction. According to CMS projections—the administration's own projections—government will pay 50 percent of healthcare costs by 2020.

Once the Obama health law enrolls millions more people in its new entitlements, how will it limit demand and control spending? The answer is by lowering the standard of care for everyone and compelling Americans who already had insurance to do with less. That is why the new health law imposes so many controls on your doctor and your insurer.

5. Americans should settle for Europe's standard of medical care. On June 1, 2009, the president's Council of Economic Advisors issued a report pointing to Europe's skimpier healthcare consumption and urging Americans to copy it.[10] But the truth is, 90 percent of the difference in per capita healthcare spending is due to higher incomes in the U.S. Greater wealth, not more waste, is the cause.[11]

Americans earn more so they spend more.

Unfortunately, many of the key architects of the Obama health law were admirers of Europe's scarcity model. David Blumenthal, for example, National Coordinator for Health Information Technology from 2009 to 2011, extolled the advantages of top-down government controls to limit consumption.[12]

Members of Congress and other Washington elites are misled by bogus claims that the U.S. spends the most for healthcare and gets little for it.

Former Senator Tom Daschle, an early spokesman for President Obama's health reform plans, told *Meet the Press* in August 2009 that Americans were spending too much and getting poor-quality healthcare. "The World Health Organization listed us 37th just below Costa Rica and above Slovenia," he said.[13]

Mainstream media outlets bought into that preposterous ranking and disseminated it far and wide. It was repeated on CNN's *Larry King Live*,[14] and the *Tampa Bay Times* even cited it to rebut Senator John McCain's claim that the U.S. has the best healthcare system in the world.[15]

Anyone who cared about the truth would have looked into how the WHO arrived at its thirty-seventh-place ranking for the United States. WHO ranked the U.S. number one on the only measure that counts: "Responsiveness to the needs of the patient." But on other measures, such as "Financial fairness" and "Health distribution," WHO gave the high marks to countries where the government pays for all healthcare and where equality reigns—with all patients receiving equally poor care.[16] What mattered to the WHO rankers were socialism and other ideological priorities—not whether a patient gets needed treatment to survive cancer.

The truth about the WHO ranking came out on April 22, 2010, one month after the Obama health law was signed. Dr. Philip Musgrove, editor in chief of the WHO report, announced in the *New England Journal of Medicine*, that it was "long past time for this zombie number [37] to disappear from circulation." He added that "there are sound reasons to mistrust the conceptual framework behind the estimates."[17]

Thank you, Dr. Musgrove, but it's a bit late.

The stakes are high and they are not political. All Americans want the best healthcare for their families. Right now, if you are seriously ill, the best place to be is in the United States. A man diagnosed with prostate cancer has a 99 percent chance of surviving it in the U.S. It is not a death sentence here. But in Europe, nearly one out of every four men diagnosed with prostate cancer dies from it.[18]

And if someone in your family has what is currently considered an "incurable" illness, America is still the nation of hope. This is where the cures are developed. Since 1950, scientists working in the United States have won more Nobel Prizes in medicine and physiology than the entire rest of the world combined.

Nobel Prize Winners in Medicine, by Country of Affiliation, 1950 to 2013

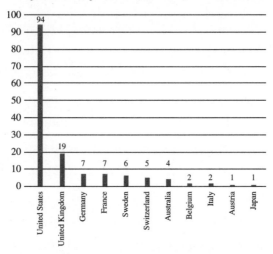

Between 1950 and 2013, the Nobel Prize in Medicine was awarded to 148 Laureates—ninety-four of them working exclusively at American institutions.

Source: Nobel Prize website, "All Nobel Laureates in Physiology or Medicine," http://www.nobelprize.org/nobel_prizes/medicine/laureates/index.html.

CHAPTER THIRTEEN

BEATING OBAMACARE

Facts You Need to Know:

- A majority of Americans already favored repealing Obamacare on election day in 2012
- What the nation needs to improve health insurance is a twenty-page bill in plain honest English
- *Any* bill passed by Congress must apply to members of Congress

This book is not about politics. It's about protecting your health, your income, and your freedom. But politics got us into this mess, and we will have to use politics to get us out of it.

The 2012 presidential election was expected to be a referendum on the Affordable Care Act. But despite the unpopularity of the law, voters reelected President Obama.

In part, that's because the weasels who wrote Obamacare postponed the pain until after the 2012 election. They put the popular provisions into effect immediately, such as allowing children to stay on their parent's plan until age twenty-six, offering "free" colonoscopies and mammograms (in truth, forcing you to pay for them in your premium, whether you get them or not), and giving women the thrill of getting contraceptives at the drugstore without paying anything.

The White House also granted 1,472 waivers to certain companies and unions exempting them from insurance reforms, so they would not drop coverage for employees and members before the presidential contest.

Voters saw through these hijinks. Even on Election Day 2012, a majority favored repealing the health law.[1] But they cared more about other issues or didn't care for Mitt Romney. The 2012 election was not a referendum on Obamacare.

Then Obamacare rolled out with a vengeance. Workers are losing their on-the-job coverage because of the rising cost of coverage. Millions of individuals lost the plans they were told they could keep. Hospitals are already laying off nurses, causing many patients to wait longer for help.

The preposterously unsuccessful rollout of Obamacare left the president's party faithful fuming. Senator Barbara Mikulski, a prominent liberal, decried the "crisis of confidence" in big-government liberalism.[2] The debacle known as Obamacare proved to Americans that the federal government couldn't launch a website, much less control one-sixth of the economy and orchestrate healthcare for all Americans. The Obamacare failure went a long way toward discrediting the notion that BIG BROTHER should run our lives.

Republicans, of course, hoped the result would favor them. Reince Priebus, chairman of the Republican National Committee, said on CNN's *State of the Union* program that the health law would be "toxic" for Democrats in future elections. "We will tattoo it to their foreheads in 2014," he said. "We will run on it. And they will lose because of it."[3]

That sentiment underestimates just how disgusted Americans of all political persuasions are with Congress and Washington, D.C., in general.

Enough Shame to Go Around

Nothing better symbolizes the cause of that disgust than the special subsidy for members of Congress to help them pay for their Obamacare premiums. The real class divide in America is between the governing class and everybody else.

Republicans and Democrats who could agree on almost nothing else connived to exempt themselves and their staff from Section 1312(d)(3)(D) of the Affordable Care Act that requires them to get their health insurance on the exchange and pay the same premiums the public will have to pay.[4]

Before 2014, members of Congress and their staff were covered by plans they chose through the Federal Employees Health Benefit Program, with taxpayers picking up around 75 percent of the tab.[5] The thinking behind the new requirement was that what's good enough for the public ought to be good enough for Congress.

Sadly, Washington lawmakers got cold feet. By August of 2013, they were claiming that even with their generous salaries (members earn $174,000 base pay), they can't afford Obamacare premiums. So the president enlisted the help of the Office of Personnel Management to arrange a back-room deal for members and their staff. Members say they're entitled because Obamacare forced them to give up their on-the-job coverage. Join the club. That's exactly what is happening to millions of other Americans.[6]

Congress needs a refresher course on the U.S. Constitution and the principles that make this nation free.

Principle 1: What's good for the goose is good for the gander. In *The Federalist* No. 57, James Madison, the chief architect of the Constitution, explained that the new nation would remain free only so long as lawmakers had to live by the same laws they imposed on the public.

Principle 2: In this nation, the rule of law is king, not Mr. Obama. Nothing in the law permits Obama to arrange taxpayer-funded subsidies for lawmakers and staff. Only Congress can appropriate the people's money to fund such subsidies.

To get rid of Obamacare, first we must get rid of the special treatment for members of Congress, which shields them from the reality of this law.

Replacing the Obama Health Law with Something Better

Conceding the shortcomings of the current flock of politicians, here are the principles that should guide us as we replace Obamacare. The goal—helping the uninsured—is important. But Obamacare lowers your standard of care, puts government in charge of your care, and takes away something as precious as life itself—your liberty. There is a better way to help the uninsured.

We need a twenty-page bill in plain English that members of Congress will read before voting on it. Don't fall for the argument that we need a "comprehensive" bill. In Washington, D.C., "comprehensive" means unread.

We need honest accounting of what the bill will cost. Almost always, the forecasts turn out to be a mere sliver of the actual cost. Americans know that the nation faces a dual crisis of excessive spending and excessive debt. We need to get the spending under control. Government spending on healthcare (including Obamacare) and Social Security are on track to consume more than half the federal budget by the end of the decade. Repealing Obamacare is vital. The best way to reform entitlements is not to create new ones.

We need to recognize that people are smart enough to make their own decisions. Obamacare was built on the premise that we are too stupid to decide what kind of health insurance we want and can afford. The "Washington knows best" crowd created a one-size-fits-all plan and tried to force everyone to buy it. But the sixty-year-old couple didn't want to pay for maternity coverage. And the young single man didn't want a health plan that paid for a vast array of services. Surprise!

Here is the summary of a twenty-page bill in plain English that will reduce premiums, help laid-off Americans afford coverage, and stay out of our private medical affairs.

Every day, Americans tell me they want a healthcare bill written in plain English.

They want members of Congress to read it before voting on it. And they want a bill that helps make insurance affordable and fair, without the federal government bludgeoning doctors and patients into accepting one-size-fits-all medical care.

Some states have taken smart approaches to lowering costs and expanding access, including helping people with pre-existing conditions. The twenty-page bill summarized below copies the reforms that have worked in those states.

To read the bill in its entirety, plus cost estimates for its implementation, visit betsymccaughey.com.

This Bill Is Not Dangerous to Your Health—or Your Freedom
(Here's what genuine health reform would look like.)

Title I

Title I liberates consumers to buy policies from insurance brokers in other states and puts consumers on notice that the products they buy outside their own state may have different benefits and consumer protections from those required by their state. This title also imposes federal consumer protections on plans sold interstate, to make sure that consumers who have paid their premiums are protected from rescission—that is, from being dropped from the plan when they get sick. These federal protections will also guarantee that adult children could stay on their parent's plan until age twenty-six, for an additional premium.

Before Obamacare, an HMO plan cost a twenty-five-year-old California male $260 a month, while a New Yorker of the same age had to pay $1,228 for a similar plan.[7] This bill would liberate the young New Yorker to buy a plan wherever he can get the best deal.

Title II

Title II provides federal incentives for states to establish medical courts, ensuring quicker, fairer verdicts in medical liability cases and at the same time preserving every litigant's right to trial by jury. Medical courts will be presided over by judges who know the issues, have experience with medical liability, and can distinguish the honest expert witnesses from the charlatan hired guns. Tort law has always been a matter left to the states. This bill does not mandate that states establish medical courts or attempt to federalize tort law. It does provide block grants to states to impose caps on damages—and more importantly, to establish medical courts. Why only cap unjust damage awards when you can go far toward eliminating them with expert medical malpractice judges?

Title III

Title III provides federal incentives for states to establish or improve subsidized high-risk pools to help consumers with pre-existing conditions.

Title IV

Title IV extends the 65 percent COBRA subsidy (from the Consolidated Omnibus Budget Reconciliation Act of 1985) established by the American Recovery and Reinvestment Act of 2009. Democrats and Republicans can find common ground here. COBRA subsidies are not a permanent entitlement, but rather temporary assistance for those who have been laid off. COBRA premiums, which laid-off workers can pay to maintain their health insurance, are costly just when a family is laid low by unemployment. For more than half the uninsured in the United States, being uninsured is a temporary problem. They find another job and have employment-based insurance again within a year. We need to help them in between jobs.

Now when you're told that Obamacare was passed because "something had to be done," you'll know there's a better way to help the uninsured. In the meantime, I hope you find this guide to the new law helpful.

THE OBAMACARE CALENDAR

Facts You Need to Know:

- Obamacare contains twenty new taxes or tax hikes, the first of which went into effect in 2010
- In 2018, the Independent Payment Advisory Board has the power to further cut what Medicare will spend on seniors

June 15, 2009

In a speech to the American Medical Association, President Obama says "no matter how we reform health care, we will keep this promise: If you like your doctor, you will be able to keep your doctor. Period. If you like your health care plan, you will be able to keep your health care plan. Period. No one will take it away. No matter what."

December 24, 2009

The Senate passes H.R. 3590, the Patient Protection and Affordable Care Act. Vote: 58 Democrats and 2 independents in favor, 39 Republicans against.

March 9, 2010

House Speaker Nancy Pelosi says: "We have to pass the bill so that you can find out what is in it."

March 21, 2010

The House of Representatives passes the bill. Two hundred nineteen Democrats vote for it, while 178 Republicans and 34 Democrats vote no.

March 23, 2010

President Obama signs the Affordable Care Act into law.

March 23, 2010

States sue, challenging the constitutionality of Obamacare. Eventually twenty-six states will join the lawsuit.

July 1, 2010

The first of twenty new taxes and tax hikes goes into effect—a 10 percent tax on tanning salons.

September 2010

Early provisions require insurers to

- eliminate co-pays for preventive care (the cost is included in your premium instead),
- cover young adults on their parent's plan until age twenty-six, and
- stop selling mini-med plans that cap the dollar amounts paid for care.

January 2011

The "Donut Hole" begins to close for Medicare Part D. New Penalties for HSA disbursements kick in. New fees on pharmaceutical companies start.

January 2012

The Obama administration discloses that over 1,200 waivers have been granted from Obamacare requirements. Most of the waivers went to labor unions.

June 28, 2012

The United States Supreme Court rules the individual mandate constitutional, citing Congress' power to tax, but says each state can decide whether or not to expand Medicaid.

January 1, 2013

Medicare Part A payroll tax hike and new 3.8 percent unearned income tax go into effect, affecting 2.5 million households.

Annual contributions to Flexible Spending Accounts are capped at $2,500.

A new 2.3 percent excise tax is imposed on medical device manufacturers.

June 27, 2013

A federal appeals court rules that Obama administration regulations requiring birth control and abortifacient drug coverage on all employee insurance plans are an unconstitutional violation of the religious rights of the owners of retailer Hobby Lobby. The case will likely reach the Supreme Court.

July 2, 2013

The Obama administration reveals it will delay enforcement of the employer mandate until 2015, contrary to the letter of the law.

October 1, 2013

Healthcare.gov is launched but collapses.

October 22, 2013

A lawsuit challenging the Obamacare subsidies in federal insurance exchanges is allowed to proceed in federal court. The suit argues that the legislation does not allow federal subsidies for insurance policies bought on the federal exchanges—the only way consumers can buy individual policies in thirty-four states.

November 1, 2013

The Obama administration announces that only 106,000 people have signed up for health plans—including just 27,000 on the federal exchange.

By this time, millions of Americans have received notices cancelling their individual health insurance plans.

November 14, 2013

The president dispenses with Section 2702 of the Affordable Care Act, meaning health plans do not have to include ten essential health benefits.

The president has changed the Affordable Care Act in many ways, and more changes could be ahead. Here is what's scheduled to happen next.

January 1, 2014

New plans under the Health Care Insurance Exchanges go into effect.

Insurers are no longer allowed to deny coverage based on pre-existing conditions; health plans are barred from placing annual limits on covered medical costs.

March 31, 2014

All Americans are required to have government-mandated insurance by this date or pay a penalty (originally scheduled for January 1, 2014).

January 1, 2015

The employer mandate (originally scheduled for January 2014) is supposed to take effect.

The penalties for failure to have government-approved health insurance rise to $325 or 2.0 percent of income.

New limits on out-of-pocket costs for individuals are imposed.

January 1, 2016

Penalties increase again for individuals without health insurance, to $695 or 2.5 percent of income.

January 1, 2018

Independent Payment Advisory Board (IPAB) powers go into effect.

The "Cadillac tax" penalizes generous health plans.

WHO GAINS
AND WHO LOSES

Facts You Need to Know:

- Unions got an airtight "grandfather clause" guaranteeing they could keep their plans until their contracts expired (Section 1251(d)). But non-union people saw their plans cancelled
- Insurance brokers are being driven out of business. The law says individuals who need coverage can qualify for subsidies only if they buy through the exchanges instead of through a broker
- Lawyers are big winners. This law is a full-employment program for constitutional lawyers. And Obamacare contains no tort reform

Winners

Low-income childless adults who were not eligible for Medicaid under the old rules may be eligible in 2014 in states that choose to expand Medicaid eligibility.

Households earning up to $92,200 for a family of four who pay for their own insurance will get a subsidy funded by taxpayers.

Young adults are now eligible to stay on their parent's health plan until age twenty-six.

Newcomers to the U.S. are also winners. The law expands programs to serve people of diverse languages and cultures, regardless of immigration status.

Racial and ethnic minorities will benefit from federally funded programs to train a diverse healthcare workforce and from numerous "community transformation grants" targeted explicitly at minority organizations.

Government employees are winners. Obamacare is causing the federal government to add workers at a rapid pace. Federal actuaries predict that government spending on healthcare administration—bureaucrats telling patients and doctors what to do—will soar from $29 billion in 2008 to more than $71 billion in 2020.

Insurance companies are both winners and losers. They are guaranteed customers. The law forces you to buy their product. But on February 29, 2012, Secretary of Health and Human Services Kathleen Sebelius told Congress the private insurance market is in a "death spiral."[1] Blame Obamacare's costly regulations.

Chronically ill patients are winners and losers. They will benefit from rules barring insurers from putting life-time caps on their care. But they will be vulnerable to the impact of funding cuts to hospitals and dialysis centers.

Losers

Millions of Americans who liked their health plans but have seen them cancelled are losers.

Nurses and other hospital employees will lose out. Hospitals will face severe budgetary pressures, warned former Chief Actuary Richard Foster, because of cuts in Medicare reimbursement. In the past, when Medicare cut payments to hospitals, nursing care was spread thinner, and nursing workloads increased.

Hospital patients will wait longer when cutbacks reduce the supply of diagnostic equipment and fewer nurses are on the floor.

Taxpayers who earn more than $200,000, or $250,000 per couple are hit with higher Medicare Part A payroll taxes and a new 3.8 percent tax on unearned income in addition to the capital gains tax.

Union members and other people with generous health plans will risk losing them in 2018, when a 40 percent "Cadillac tax" on insurers offering these plans begins.

Doctors can expect lower pay, more paperwork, and more government interference in how they treat their patients.

Seniors pay for more than half the Obama health law through cuts in Medicare and Medicare Advantage programs. They will get less care than if the law hadn't passed. Baby boomers will enter Medicare in record numbers over the next decade. They will also get less care than if the law had not passed.

Young healthy people who sign up for Obamacare plans will be paying high premiums to subsidize the costs of older, sicker people.

Women (and men) who want to keep their medical records private will find it hard to do so. Privacy advocates claim the law will compel Americans to share "with millions of strangers who are not physicians confidential private and personal medical history information they do not wish to share."[2]

THE OBAMACARE DICTIONARY

Abortion: The Obama health law says that federally subsidized health plans can offer abortion coverage, but must set up separate accounts to segregate federal funds from money used for abortions. Before the law was enacted, Congressman Joe Pitts (Pennsylvania Republican) and Congressman Bart Stupak (Michigan Democrat) called segregating funds "an accounting gimmick" and proposed an amendment to ban abortions in all federally subsidized health plans.

The Senate majority resisted the amendment, and the president succeeded in getting the health law passed without it. He offered instead an executive order reaffirming the Hyde Amendment, a 1976 provision named after the late Representative Henry Hyde (Illinois Republican) that bans federal funds for abortions except in the cases of rape and incest, and to protect the life of the mother.

An executive order depends on the whim of the president and can be changed at any time, pro-life forces argue. In October 2011, pro-life lawmakers tried again for a statute to bar a health plan from offering abortion coverage if any enrollees receive federal subsidies. It passed the House 251–172 but was not taken up in the Senate. In conclusion, whether abortions are funded through federal programs such as community health centers will depend on the discretion of the president and the Secretary of Health and Human Services. The law does not address the issue.

Accountable Care Organizations: On December 19, 2011, Secretary of Health and Human Services Kathleen Sebelius unveiled the first thirty-two Accountable Care Organizations or ACOs designed to reduce Medicare costs. ACOs are groups of doctors and other healthcare providers, usually including a hospital, that agree to coordinate how they treat a patient with the goal of reducing costs. Coordination might mean shortening hospital stays, for example. Each ACO will treat five thousand or more Medicare patients. If the ACO reduces costs, each caregiver gets a bonus from the federal government. The less it costs to care for a senior, the more doctors and hospitals earn. As of October 2013, there were 370 ACOs around the country, and 150 more in the pipeline.[1]

American Indians: Attached to the Obamacare legislation is a reauthorization of the Indian Health Care Improvement Act, which was first passed in 1976 and last reauthorized in 2000. The Obama health law makes it permanent and expands services to American Indians, including Alaskan tribes and urban Indians. The expansion includes more mental and behavioral health services and dialysis.

Annual Caps: Starting in 2014, the health law bans annual limits on what your insurance plan will pay out when you need care.

Automatic Enrollment: Employers with more than two hundred full-time workers will be required to automatically enroll their employees into health plans. Employees can opt out, but employers have no choice. The Obama administration expects to finish drafting regulations on this subject in 2014, and until then this requirement is on hold.[2]

Breast Cancer in Young Women Initiative: Section 399NN of the law directs the Centers for Disease Control and Prevention to create an educational campaign focused on breast cancer awareness in women ages fifteen to forty-four and directs the National Institutes of Health to develop new screening tests to detect breast cancer in young women. Widespread screening by current methods is impractical, it is said, because so few younger women contract breast cancer. Only about 10 percent of the approximately 250,000 women diagnosed each year with breast cancer are younger than forty-five, according to the American Cancer Society. Therefore a different approach is needed to identify those young women at risk of the disease.

Cadillac Tax: In 2018, if you are enrolled in a plan costing at least $10,200 a year ($27,500 for family coverage), your insurance company will be taxed 40 percent for selling you that plan.[3] The Cadillac tax is an excise tax on insurers, and it is designed to penalize and discourage some people from having better or more high-end coverage than everybody else. But remember, limits on what you can pay for insurance also limit what is in the pot to take care of you when you're sick. This tax is also a major source of revenue to pay for the health law.

Centers for Medicare & Medicaid Services (CMS): A division of the Department of Health and Human Services.

Community Health Centers: The Obama health law provides $11 billion in additional funding for community health centers. The centers are intended to serve largely the uninsured, especially illegal immigrants, according to HHS officials.[4]

Community Transformation Grants: Section 4201 of the health law empowers the Centers for Disease Control and Prevention (CDC) to hand out grants to local organizations that propose to improve the emotional and social wellness of their community, combat environmental hazards, foster healthy living, and reduce health disparities between races. In 2011, the CDC awarded $103 million in community transformation grants, and it continues to make new grants. The total for 2012 was $70 million.[5]

In September 2012, $7.9 million was awarded to Community Health Councils, based in Los Angeles, California. That's a large amount for an organization that claims to have a $2 million annual budget. On September 26, the organization posted a long list of job openings.

Community Health Councils' mission is "to promote social justice" and ensure more health and community resources go to people of color. However, for more than a decade, executive director Lark Galloway-Gilliam has led protests under the organization's banner against fracking, for-profit hospitals, and state budget cuts and has partnered with the Natural Resources Defense Council to file lawsuits against oil drilling.

Community Health Councils says part of the $7.9 million will be used to "educate community members on environmental hazards," and 65 percent will be distributed to its community partners. One partner is Los Angeles Community Action Network, which, according to its mission statement, "promotes voter engagement as a means of civic participation" and conducts "one-on-one education in the streets" as well as "monthly teach-ins for downtown residents." Other partners include tenants' rights advocates, anti-fracking and anti-drilling groups, church groups, and one actual health advocacy group, Families in Good Health.[6]

Comparative Effectiveness Research: Even before the enactment of the Obama health law, Congress approved $1.1 billion in the stimulus law (2009) to create a new government agency called the Federal Coordinating Council for Comparative Effectiveness Research. Fifteen government officials appointed by the president will oversee evaluations of what medications and treatments work best. Almost all medical journal articles already compare effectiveness—which medication or which treatment approach works better. And of course, more research is better than less. But many doctors are concerned that this federal effort at standardization will lead to cookie-cutter guidelines at a time when new discoveries are pointing in the opposite direction—to the advantages of personalized medicine based on the patient's individual genetic make-up. Doctors also worry that the conclusions of the agency will eventually lead to limitations on which treatments are paid for.

Consumer Operated and Oriented Plans (CO-OPs): Section 1322 of the Obama health law created Consumer Operated and Oriented Plans, or CO-OPs for short, to compete in each state with for-profit insurers. CO-OPs generally are funded by members, but Obamacare CO-OPs will borrow their start-up funds and reserve balances from the federal government. Administration officials predicted that even with "flexible" and "individualized" repayment plans, 40 percent of the loans for start-up costs and 35 percent of the loans for reserves will default, in part because CO-OP applicants will lack insurance experience, and their proposals will be based on untried models. Week after week leading up to the 2012 presidential election, the administration announced more of these multi-million-dollar loans to flimsy start-ups: twenty in all in twenty states, totaling $1.6 billion in government loans, with another $2.2 billion in loans budgeted. It makes the $387 million the government lost to failed energy venture Solyndra look like peanuts.[7] During the budget negotiations over the so-called "fiscal cliff" in January 2013, funding for the CO-OP program was eliminated. As a result of the funding cuts, many CO-OPs are expected to fail, meaning they are likely to default on their loans.[8]

Contraception: Nothing in the Affordable Care Act guarantees that health plans must provide contraception, sterilization, or "morning after" drugs. The law requires individual and group plans to include essential benefits, and gives the Secretary of Health and Human Services—an appointee of the president—the discretion to define them. President Barack Obama and his HHS Secretary have decreed that all health plans must cover contraception, sterilization, and morning after pills. A future occupant of the White House could decree just the opposite. (See also: **Waivers.**)

Cornhusker Kickback: In return for Democratic senator Ben Nelson's vote in favor of the healthcare reform legislation proposed by his party, Nelson's home state of Nebraska was promised special treatment that would allow Nebraska taxpayers to avoid paying for newly eligible Medicaid enrollees. When news of the deal became public it triggered widespread outrage, with the loudest protests coming from Arnold Schwarzenegger, the only Republican governor to support Obamacare. He demanded that California and every other state in the country get the same deal given to Nebraska. In the end that's what happened.[9]

Cultural Competency Training: Section 5307 of the law requires the Secretary of Health and Human Services to support grants and demonstration projects to promote cultural competency training for nurses and other health professionals.

Dependents: Your household dependents, meaning your children and a non-working spouse, must have health coverage. But your employer does not have to contribute to the cost of that coverage. And yet if you have "affordable" health coverage through your employer, even if it's an individual policy that covers only you, your dependents are not eligible for subsidies on the exchanges.

Disparities: In the implementation of the president's health law, the administration is committed to "reduc[ing] differences in the amount and quality of healthcare" that different racial and ethnic groups receive. According to an "Action Plan" written primarily by Assistant Secretary for Health Howard Koh and released by the Obama administration in 2010, "Although disparities can also be viewed through many other lenses—for example, socioeconomic status, sex, age, level of disability, geography, sexual orientation, or gender identity—the Action Plan focuses specifically on race and ethnicity." The Action Plan calls for updating standards for culturally and linguistically appropriate services, training healthcare interpreters, and developing new software and other technologies to help people with limited English proficiency enroll in Medicaid.[10]

Doctor Shortage: The Association of American Medical Colleges predicts a shortage of 160,000 doctors by 2025.[11] The Physicians Foundation did a survey at the end of 2010 and concluded that the shortage may become even larger as physicians unhappy with the new health law retire early.[12]

Donut Hole: The prescription drug coverage gap in Medicare Part D. Most prescription drug purchases are covered up until a limit, currently $2,800. Then the senior is on the hook for 100 percent of any further drug purchases until he reaches the catastrophic level of $6,400 in drug purchases in a single year, at which point Medicare Part D pays 95 percent. About one out of four Medicare recipients gets stuck in the donut hole and has to pay the whole cost of some drug purchases. The Obama health law slowly closes the donut hole. (See Chapter Seven above.)

Dual Eligibles: People who qualify for Medicare and Medicaid are called dual eligible. They number approximately ten million, and they are generally the highest-cost patients supported by public insurance. The Obama health law creates a new Federal Coordinated Health Care office within the Department of Health and Human Services to better coordinate their care and control its costs.

Emergency Medicaid: This is available to any person whose acute symptoms must be treated, and whose income falls below 133 percent of the federal poverty line, regardless of the person's immigration status.

Emergency Medical Treatment and Active Labor Act: Passed in 1986, this federal law bars hospitals from denying emergency medical care, including childbirth services, to *anyone* who needs care.

Employer Mandate: Any employer with fifty or more full-time employees has to offer what the government deems "essential coverage" or pay a fine based on the number of full-time employees. This requirement has now been postponed by the president for a year, until January 1, 2015, and it may never go into effect. (See Chapter Four above.)

Enroll America: Enroll America is a tax-exempt non-profit organization formed to maximize enrollment in Obamacare programs, including Medicaid and the plans on the exchanges. It creates training materials for navigators, public relations campaigns for exchanges, and partners with community activists. It is staffed largely by former Obama campaign staffers and former Obama White House staff.

Essential Health Care Benefits: Beginning in 2014, the Obama health law requires everyone to have health insurance that includes "essential health care benefits," as defined by the Secretary of Health and Human Services and state lawmakers. Secretary Sebelius defined these "essential benefits" to include contraception and maternity care (even for women over seventy years old, and for men) and substance-abuse treatment (even for people who never drink or do drugs). Because of this requirement, millions of Americans lost their health insurance policies and discovered the new policies now available were much more expensive, so President Obama announced that insurers could continue to offer non-compliant plans to those who previously had them, but not to new customers.

Exchanges: Section 1311 of the healthcare law states that each state "shall establish an American Health Benefit Exchange." Generally individuals who do not get on-the-job coverage were supposed to be able to go to a website to buy a "qualified" health plan. Fourteen states and Washington, D.C., chose to set up exchanges, and in the remaining thirty-six states the federal government is operating its own exchanges.[13]

Exemption Certificate: Some people are exempt from the individual mandate, including American Indians, members of certain religious groups, and people with very low incomes. But to receive the exemption, the Healthcare.gov website advises you to "fill out an exemption application in the Marketplace." Unfortunately, the exemption application form is nowhere to be found on the Healthcare.gov website.[14] You can also claim your exemption from the individual mandate when you file your annual tax return.[15]

Federal Data Hub: If you buy health insurance on any Obamacare exchange, you will have to provide personal information such as your Social Security number, citizenship status, income level, and date of birth. This sensitive information goes into a huge Federal Data Hub, which links the Social Security Administration, Justice

Department, Homeland Security, the IRS, and state agencies. Will your information be protected? The countless flaws in the website's rollout have led many to fear that their data won't be secure. In fact, the fine print on the website warns consumers that they "have no reasonable expectation of privacy."

Health Disparities Data Collection: Section 4302 of the law requires the Secretary of Health and Human Services to ensure that all federally supported health programs collect and report data on race, ethnicity, sex, primary language, and disability status to help reduce disparities in health and healthcare.

Health Savings Accounts (HSAs): Tax-advantaged accounts available to taxpayers who are enrolled in high-deductible health plans. They began in 2003. If you have an HSA you can contribute part of your income to it, without paying income tax on it, and allow the funds to roll over year to year in the account until you need them to pay for medical expenses. Proponents think HSAs encourage individuals to be more responsible for their healthcare expenses and more conscious of cost. The Obama health law puts HSAs at a disadvantage because the new law requires that you pay for all preventive care up front in your premium (rather than from your Health

Savings Account when you are actually treated). Also the new health law caps deductibles at $2,000, which is about one-third of what is currently allowed. Finally the new health law bars you from using your HSA funds to pay for over-the-counter drugs, unless you get a doctor's prescription for them.

Hobby Lobby: Hobby Lobby, an arts and crafts retailer, is one of many private companies that filed First Amendment challenges to Obamacare. The store's owners, who are devout Christians, contend that the Obama administration's requirement that employee health plans cover abortion drugs conflicts with their First Amendment right to practice their religion. The Supreme Court has announced it will hear the case.

Independent Payment Advisory Board (IPAB): An unelected board empowered to reduce what doctors and hospitals are paid. With the creation of IPAB, Congress has surrendered decisions about Medicare spending to unelected bureaucrats, who are not accountable to the voters. (See Chapters Seven and Ten above.)

Medicaid: A government health program for people with low incomes. Medicaid is a means-tested program established in 1965. Until the changes to Medicaid made by

Obamacare, the Medicaid program was managed primarily by state governments, which determined eligibility standards and benefits to fit what their own taxpayers and budgets could handle. In 1997, Congress added CHIP, the Children's Health Insurance Program. (See Chapter Six above.)

Medical Loss Ratio: Health insurers selling plans to individuals and small groups will have to spend 80 percent of premiums collected on medical benefits. Plans sold to large groups will have to spend 85 percent on medical benefits. Plans that fail to meet that standard will have to refund some premium revenue to their enrollees.

Medical Malpractice: Despite urgent pleas from physicians, the Obama health law does little to address the high costs of medical malpractice insurance and the costly defensive medicine doctors use to shield themselves from unfair lawsuits. Obamacare awards five-year demonstration grants to states to develop remedies for out-of-control malpractice lawsuits. Critics of this approach would argue that some states, notably Texas, have already proven what works. These states have already developed successful strategies—including caps on non-economic and punitive damages, and special medical courts—that need to be expanded nationwide.

Medical Tax Deductions: Obamacare limits deductions for medical expenses. Through 2012 you can deduct expenses that exceed 7.5 percent of your adjusted gross income. Starting in 2013, that threshold rises to 10 percent.

Medicare: A national health insurance program for seniors and the disabled administered by the federal government. Medicare guarantees access to healthcare for Americans age sixty-five and older and the disabled of all ages. Medicare has four parts: Part A provides hospital care insurance; Part B covers doctors visits, home healthcare, and hospice care. Part D, added by Congress in 2006, provides coverage for medications. Part C, also called Medicare Advantage, allows seniors to participate in private health plans instead of the government-run system. All citizens are eligible, as are legal residents who have been in the U.S. for five years. (See Chapter Seven above.)

Medicare Advantage Plans: Under Medicare Part C, about one-quarter of seniors enroll in Medicare Advantage Plans offered by a wide array of private insurers. The Obama health law reduces what the federal government pays to subsidize these plans, and already many plans have dropped doctors and benefits—or stopped offering coverage to seniors altogether. (See Chapter Seven above.)

Medicare Payroll Tax: Starting in 2013, if you earn more than $200,000 (or you and your spouse earn more than $250,000), your share of the tax went up from 1.45 percent of your gross income to 2.35 percent. Despite the name of the tax, the additional money does not go to Medicare.

Medicare Tax on "Unearned" Income: Starting in 2013, if you sell your home or another investment and make a profit, or get "unearned income" from dividends, interest, and other sources, you have to pay a 3.8 percent tax on the gain, in addition to capital gains tax if you are a high earner. A high earner is defined as anyone having an adjusted gross income above $200,000 (or $250,000 for a couple). Warning: you may not earn that much yearly, but if the profit from your home sale, added to your annual income, pushes you into that category, your profit will incur this new 3.8 percent tax. Sales of primary residences are exempt up to $500,000 in some circumstances.

Navigators: As of October 2013, over 2,000 "navigators" had been hired by community organizations, unions, and community health centers, nominally to assist Americans in signing up for coverage on the Obamacare exchanges. Taxpayer funds provide the grants to these organizations to hire the navigators the first year. In subsequent years, the money to pay them comes out of premiums. In August

2013, thirteen state attorneys general complained to the Obama administration that navigators are not being properly screened. A few states, including Texas and Florida, have instituted criminal background checks.[16] (See also: **Enroll America**.)

Nutritional Labeling: Section 4206 of the Obama health law requires that all chain restaurants with twenty or more locations, and also vending machine operators, post caloric information next to each food or beverage, including each alcoholic beverage, sold. The requirement will apply even to salad bars, buffet lines, and cafeterias.

Dieters will be grateful, but business owners are complaining about the cost of redoing signs every time they add a new item to their menu. Domino's Pizza estimates this requirement could cost each of its franchisees as much as $4,700 a year.[17] The FDA estimates compliance costs could exceed $500 million. As of November 2013, the final regulations were still pending.[18]

Observation Care: If you are a senior on Medicare, beware of this: when it is not clear that an ill patient needs to be hospitalized, the patient may not—technically—be actually admitted to the hospital but rather placed under "observation" within the hospital, often in the emergency room. Too often, elderly patients are held "under observation" for two or three days, or more—because the hospital staff are gaming the reimbursement system. The Obama health law penalizes hospitals based on how much they spend on Medicare patients and especially for readmitting them for a second hospital stay. Hospital staff may try to avoid these penalties by keeping an ill senior "under observation." The financial problems for the patients are manifold. "Under observation" doesn't count as hospitalized, so a patient under observation is not eligible for nursing home care when discharged. Also, costs for being "under observation" at a hospital are paid by Medicare Part B instead of Part A, which means larger out-of-pocket costs for the patient. Some Medicare advocacy groups are actually suing to stop the Department of Health and Human Services from allowing "under observation" status.

Origination Clause: Under the Constitution (Article I, Section 7, Clause 1), all laws that raise federal revenue must originate in the House of Representatives. A pending federal lawsuit argues that the Affordable Care Act, which contains numerous taxes, unconstitutionally originated in the U.S. Senate.

Out-of-Pocket Expenses: Obamacare sets a cap on out-of-pocket expenses under all health insurance plans purchased on the exchanges. In 2014 the maximum that consumers should have to pay out of pocket will be $6,350 for individuals and $12,700 for families. Caps on out-of-pocket expenses for group health plans were postponed by the president.

Parental Coverage: Starting in September 2010, the law required health plans to cover the "children" of policyholders until age twenty-six. Previously, coverage for children ended at age nineteen, or a few years later for full-time students.[19]

Part-Time Workers: The Affordable Care Act defines part-time workers as those working fewer than thirty hours a week. During 2013, the "look back" period on which the government would calculate employers' full-time workforce for the purposes of determining their compliance with the employer mandate, employers aggressively cut workers' hours to avoid Obamacare mandates and penalties. Seventy-seven percent of hires in the first half of 2013 were of part-time workers.

Promotores: Defined by HHS as "trusted local people who serve as community health workers," promotores, the Obama administration recently announced, will be trained by a National Steering Committee to bring benefits to underserved groups.[20]

Rating Bands: Before the Obama health law, insurers in many states gave young people a big price break. The average twenty-five-year-old man uses only about a quarter as much healthcare as a fifty-five-year-old man. But the Obama health law compels insurers to stay within certain rating bands, limiting the price break that young people can get. The idea is to compel young people to subsidize the cost of care for the middle-aged. The two escapes for young adults are to stay on their parent's policy or sign up for a high-deductible plan allowed only for people under thirty.

Reasonable Break Time for Nursing Mothers: Section 4207 of the Obama health law amends Section 7 of the Fair Labor Standards Act to require employers to provide a reasonable break time for an employee to express breast milk for her nursing child for up to one year after the child's birth. The employer must also provide a space, other than a bathroom, that is shielded from view and free from intrusion by co-workers and the public.

Refund Offset: This is the only IRS collection method allowed under the Obama health law. The government may not use liens, issue levies and other penalties, or institute criminal proceedings against those who fail to enroll in a "qualified plan" or pay the penalty. Eventually people will realize that if they don't have a refund coming, the government can't collect the penalties. Thus some people may adjust their tax withholding to avoid a refund.

Reinsurance Fee: Obamacare mandates a reinsurance fee on insurance issuers and self-insured plans, with the revenue going toward "transitional reinsurance programs." The fee is expected to generate $12 billion in revenue in 2014, $8 billion in 2015, and $5 billion in 2016. Reinsurance programs are designed to compensate insurers who get a disproportionate number of sick enrollees.[21] Responding to pressure from unions, the Obama administration announced in October 2013 that it might exempt certain union plans from paying the fee.[22] (See also: **Self-Insured.**)

Secretary of Health and Human Services (HHS): Aside from the President of the United States, this is the person who will be making all the important decisions about your health: what your plan covers, what you have to pay, even what your doctor can do to treat you. In the first six months after the law was passed, 4,105 pages of new regulations were issued,[23] mostly from Health and Human Services and the new commissions, boards, and panels that report to the Secretary of HHS. There are over a thousand places where the law says, "The Secretary shall...."

Self-Employed: If you work for yourself, you will be eligible to buy the mandatory coverage on the exchange in your state.

Self-Insured: Many companies pay employees' health costs directly instead of contracting with an insurance company. This approach, known as self-insurance, offers companies greater flexibility at lower cost, and avoids some of the requirements and taxes imposed under Obamacare. Sixty-one percent of employees covered at work are in self-insured plans, according to the Kaiser Family Foundation. The *Wall Street Journal* recently warned that liberals are hoping to clamp down on self-insurance, making it less feasible for small employers to self-insure so more of their workers will be pushed into Obamcare exchange plans. (See also: **Reinsurance Fee.**)

Small Business Tax Credits: The new law offers tax credits to small businesses to offer health insurance, provided the employer covers at least 50 percent of the premium for the worker (not necessarily for family coverage). To qualify for the full credit (35 percent of the employer's cost), the business must have ten or fewer workers and an average salary not higher than $25,000.[24] The program ends altogether in 2016. So far, few businesses have responded. According to a survey by the Small Business and Entrepreneurship Council, reported in *Forbes Maga-zine*, nearly 90 percent of small businesses surveyed had not applied for the tax credit.[25] The rules are rigid, the credit declines if a business expands beyond ten employ-ees, and employers may worry about how to pay for cover-age once the program expires. The Obama administration expected millions of businesses to apply for the credits, but only 170,000 claimed the discount in its first year, and just 28,000 received the full amount.[26]

Stimulus Legislation: The American Recovery and Rein-vestment Act, enacted by the 111th Congress in February 2009, contained several provisions that paved the way for the Obama health law. The most important was a $25.8 billion allocation to provide health information technol-ogy for doctors and hospitals.

Subsidies: In 2014, you will be required to have health insurance the government deems adequate. To make this requirement less onerous, the federal government (at taxpayers' expense) will offer subsidies to individuals and households making between 133 and 400 percent of the federal poverty line. Your subsidy will be paid directly to your health plan when you enroll through the exchange in your state. Or you may choose to pay the full price of your premium and receive the subsidy when you file your annual tax return.[27]

Tanning Salons: The first of eighteen new taxes or tax hikes under the law is on tanning services. You or the tanning salon owner pay a 10 percent tax on all services sold, as of July 1, 2010.

Temporary High-Risk Pool: Obamacare creates a national temporary high-risk pool to sell insurance to people with pre-existing conditions who have been uninsured for at least six months. Applications were accepted starting in July 1, 2010, with coverage beginning a month later. All U.S. citizens and legal residents are eligible. This was a temporary program, and enrollees are expected to purchase coverage on the state exchanges beginning in 2014. The health law allocated $5 billion to fund the program.

Uninsured: According to the 2010 U.S. Census, 49.9 million people said they were uninsured. But 14 million of them were already eligible for government programs such as Medicaid or CHIP (for children) and hadn't signed up. Another 7.6 million had household incomes over $75,000. That leaves about 28.3 million people who probably cannot afford insurance. About 18 million of them are

American citizens. The number of uninsured Americans fell to 48.6 million in 2011 and 48.0 million in 2012.[28] With millions of insurance cancellation letters going out to Americans whose policies didn't meet the "essential benefits" standards of the Obama health law and lower than expected enrollment in the exchanges, Obamacare may actually result in a net increase in the number of uninsured Americans.

U.S. Preventive Services Task Force (USPSTF): Section 4105(a) of the Obama health law empowers the Secretary of Health and Human Services to "modify or eliminate" certain preventive services for seniors based on the recommendations of the USPSTF. This panel of primary care providers including physicians, nurses, and behavioral health experts was founded in 1984. It has come under criticism in recent years for recommending less use of cancer screening techniques, including mammograms, on healthy and older patients. In 2012, the USPSTF recommended against PSA screening for prostate cancer.

Immediately the prostate cancer experts at the James Buchanan Brady Urological Institute at Johns Hopkins issued a warning that the USPSTF recommendation "sets the clock back to before the 1990s, when 'healthy men' were diagnosed with cancer that was palpable and often, too late for a cure." Early diagnosis, say the Hopkins experts, is "everything." Because of PSA tests, deaths from prostate cancer have plummeted 40 percent since the 1990s, and are now rare. The Hopkins experts pointed out that the USPSTF "had no urologists or other prostate cancer experts. Rather it was composed of individuals with little or no knowledge of the disease...." There is more information on this controversy at the website of the James Buchanan Brady Urological Institute at Johns Hopkins.[29]

Vitter Amendment: Louisiana Senator David Vitter (Republican) has proposed legislation that would require all members of Congress (and their office staff), the president, vice president, and all administration appointees to buy their health insurance under Obamacare's health exchanges—without any government subsidies. Obamacare already requires members of Congress and Capitol Hill staffers to buy health insurance on the exchanges, but in August 2013 the administration weaseled a special deal through the Office of Personnel Management to pay for 75 percent of the cost of a Gold plan for members of Congress. Vitter's amendment would do away with that back-door deal.

W-2: The federal form that employers send you stating your gross pay and deductions. Starting in 2012, box 12 includes the value of your employer-provided health insurance, if you work for an employer who sends out 250 or more W-2s. The IRS says the value listed in box 12 is not considered taxable income—at least for now. But there are already proposals afoot to start taxing these benefits.[30]

Waivers: These are exemptions from parts of the Obama health law granted at the pleasure of the executive branch. Before 2011, the Obama administration granted 1,472 waivers to certain companies and unions, allowing them not to comply with the new law barring low annual caps and lifetime caps on what insurance companies will pay when an enrollee becomes ill. These waivers related to annual caps on insurance payouts are supposed to expire at the beginning of 2014. Recently, the Obama administration considered but denied Catholic institutions, such as hospitals and schools, an exemption from the employer mandate requirement that all employers, even Catholics, provide coverage for contraception, sterilization, and morning after pills for their workers. Though the law does not empower the executive branch to exempt some people from these aspects of the law, the administration is taking the stand that it has the authority to do so. On July 2, 2013, the Obama administration announced that it would delay enforcement of the employer mandate by a year. On

November 14, 2013, the president announced that the "essential benefits" requirement for insurance policies under Obamacare would not be enforced until January 1, 2015. Critics say the administration's approach turns the rule of law into rule by waivers and favoritism.

ACKNOWLEDGMENTS

This book is dedicated to the physicians of the past half-century. The discoveries of that golden age of medicine have given each of us, on average, seven additional years of life. And high-quality years. Disability among the elderly has plummeted. Older people travel, play sports, and enjoy grandchildren instead of languishing in wheel chairs and nursing homes. Thank you for the wonderful gift of a longer, more active life.

A half-century ago, it was not uncommon for Americans to die in their fifties or sixties from heart disease. My own father did. At that time, heart disease killed 1.7 million Americans every year. Now, according to the National Institutes of Health, the death rate has fallen to less than a quarter of that. Physicians at bedside and researchers in labs have achieved an amazing leap in longevity for most of us.

So I thank these physicians and researchers for their dedication to patients and their relentless pursuit of treatments for heart disease and other age-related ailments.

Unfortunately this remarkable progress, fueled by costly technology and made possible by free markets and untethered physicians, is threatened by the government controls imposed by the Obama health law. That is an important reason to oppose this law and undo it.

I am indebted to talented editors at major newspapers across the country who published my discoveries about this law as I made them, especially Robert Pollock. Howard Dickman, and Matthew Lasswell at the *Wall Street Journal*, Mark Cunningham at the *New York Post*, Wes Mann and Terry Jones at *Investor's Business Daily*, and R. Emmett Tyrell at the *American Spectator*.

Also deserving of recognition (not just from me, but from the nation) are the radio and television professionals who inform their audiences about the Obama health law: Neil Cavuto, Stuart Varney, Lou Dobbs, Larry Kudlow, Tom Marr, Lars Larson, Megyn Kelley, Sean Hannity, Mark Levin, Simon Conway, Jan Michelson, Monica Crowley, Brian Tilton, Rush Limbaugh, James Golden, Rita Cosby, and Dennis Miller.

For assistance in getting this book to you—the reader—when you need it the most, I'd like to thank my colleague and friend Amber Christian most of all. Also deserving thanks are John Bennett for research assistance and the talented team at Regnery Publishing including Marji Ross, Harry Crocker, and Elizabeth Kantor.

Finally, a very personal thanks to Charles H. Brunie, whose character, devotion to liberty, and words of encouragement inspire me day after day.

Betsy McCaughey, Ph.D.
New York, New York, 2013

NOTES

Chapter One: Obamacare Will Change Everyone's Healthcare

1. "Text: Obama's Speech on Health Care Reform," *New York Times*, June 15, 2009, http://www.nytimes.com/2009/06/15/health/policy/15obama.text.html?_r=0&pagewanted=all.
2. Aaron Blake, "Obama Blames 'Bad Apple Insurers' for Canceled Insurance Plans," *Washington Post*, October 30, 2013, http://www.washingtonpost.com/blogs/post-politics/wp/2013/10/30/obama-blames-bad-apple-insurers-for-canceled-insurance-plans/.
3. Congressional Budget Office, "May 2013 Estimate of the Effects of the Affordable Care Act on Health Insurance Coverage," http://www.cbo.gov/sites/default/files/cbofiles/attachments/44190_EffectsAffordableCareActHealthInsuranceCoverage_2.pdf.
4. Shubham Singhal, Jeris Stueland, and Drew Ungerman, "How US Health Care Reform Will Affect Employee Benefits," McKinsey & Company, June 2011, http://www.mckinsey.com/insights/health_systems_and_services/how_us_health_care_reform_will_affect_employee_benefits.
5. See Watchdog.org, "Top Hospitals Opt Out of Obamacare," *U.S. News & World Report*, October 30, 2013, http://health.usnews.com/health-news/hospital-of-tomorrow/articles/2013/10/30/top-hospitals-opt-out-of-obamacare_print.html and

Watchdog.org, "Which Top Hospitals Take Your Health Insurance under Obamacare?" *U.S. News & World Report*, October 30, 2013, http://health.usnews.com/health-news/hospital-of-tomorrow/articles/2013/10/30/which-top-hospitals-take-your-health-insurance-under-obamacare.

6. Sarah Palermo, "Concord Hospital Not Part of Provider Network for Obamacare Exchange Plan in N.H.," *Concord Monitor*, September 6, 2013, http://www.concordmonitor.com/news/8366940-95/concord-hospital-not-part-of-provider-network-for-obamacare-exchange-plan-in-nh.

7. Vivian Y. Wu and Yu-Chu Chen, "The Long Term Impact of Medicare Payment Reductions on Patient Outcomes," National Bureau of Economic Research Working Paper 16859, March 2011.

8. Carl Campanile, "Elderly Patients Sick over Losing Doctors under ObamaCare," *New York Post*, October 25, 2013, http://nypost.com/2013/10/25/elderly-patients-sick-over-losing-doctors-under-obamacare/.

9. Jackie Calmes and Robert Pear, "Crucial Rule Is Delayed a Year for Obama's Health Law," *New York Times*, July 2, 2013, http://www.nytimes.com/2013/07/03/us/politics/obama-administration-to-delay-health-law-requirement-until-2015.html.

10. Centers for Medicare & Medicaid Services, "National Health Expenditure Projections 2010–2020," table 2, http://www.cms.gov/Research-Statistics-Data-and-Systems/Statistics-Trends-and-Reports/NationalHealthExpendData/downloads/proj2010.pdf.

11. Barack Obama, "Remarks by the President on the Affordable Care Act and the Government Shutdown," whitehouse.gov, October 1, 2013, http://www.whitehouse.gov/the-press-office/2013/10/01/remarks-president-affordable-care-act-and-government-shutdown.

12. Sam Baker, "HHS Grants 106 New Healthcare Waivers," Healthwatch (The Hill's healthcare blog), August 19, 2011, http://thehill.com/blogs/healthwatch/health-reform-implementation/177581-hhs-grants-106-new-healthcare-waivers.

13. James Madison, *The Federalist* No. 62, Yale Law School's Avalon Project, http://avalon.law.yale.edu/18th_century/fed62.asp.

Chapter Two: It's Mandatory

1.   "Text: Obama's Speech on Health Care Reform," *New York Times*, June 15, 2009, http://www.nytimes.com/2009/06/15/health/policy/15obama.text.html?_r=0&pagewanted=all.

2.   "The Affordable Care Act and African Americans," U.S. Department of Health and Human Services Fact Sheet, April 12, 2012 (updated September 30, 2013), http://www.hhs.gov/healthcare/facts/factsheets/2012/04/aca-and-african-americans04122012a.html.

3.   "Text: Obama's Speech on Health Care Reform," *New York Times*.

4.   See the text of the Affordable Care Act, available at the Government Printing Office website, http://www.gpo.gov/fdsys/pkg/BILLS-111hr3590enr/pdf/BILLS-111hr3590enr.pdf.

5.   Ibid.

6.   Barack Obama, "Remarks by the President on the Affordable Care Act," whitehouse.gov, September 26, 2013, http://www.whitehouse.gov/the-press-office/2013/09/26/remarks-president-affordable-care-act.

7.   See the text of the Affordable Care Act, available at the Government Printing Office website, http://www.gpo.gov/fdsys/pkg/BILLS-111hr3590enr/pdf/BILLS-111hr3590enr.pdf.

8.   John Parkinson, "IRS Official in Charge during Tea Party Targeting Now Runs Health Care Office," ABC News, May 16, 2013, http://abcnews.go.com/blogs/politics/2013/05/irs-official-in-charge-during-tea-party-targeting-now-runs-health-care-office/.

9.   For information on the legislation, the HITECH Act of 2009, see "Health IT Legislation," at HealthIT.gov, http://www.healthit.gov/policy-researchers-implementers/health-it-legislation.

10.   "New NYCLU Report Reveals Privacy Threats in Sharing of Electronic Health Records," New York Civil Liberties Union, March 6, 2012, http://www.nyclu.org/news/new-nyclu-report-reveals-privacy-threats-sharing-of-electronic-health-records.

11.   Department of Health and Human Services, "Modifications to the HIPAA Privacy, Security, Enforcement, and Breach Notification Rules under the Health Information Technology for Economic and Clinical Health Act and the Genetic Information Nondiscrimination Act; Other Modifications to the HIPAA Rules; Final Rule,"

Federal Register 78, no. 17 (January 25, 2013), http://www.gpo.gov/ fdsys/pkg/FR-2013-01-25/pdf/2013-01073.pdf. See "New Rule Protects Patient Privacy, Secures Health Information," U.S. Department of Health & Human Services news release, January 17, 2013, http://www.hhs.gov/news/press/2013pres/01/20130117b. html, which includes this statement: "When individuals pay by cash they can instruct their provider not to share information about their treatment with their health plan."

Chapter Three: Obamacare's Substandard Exchange Plans

1. Section 1311(b)1, text of the Affordable Care Act, Government Printing Office, http://www.gpo.gov/fdsys/pkg/BILLS-111hr3590enr/pdf/BILLS-111hr3590enr.pdf.

2. Jackie Farwell, "LePage Won't 'Lift a Finger' to Set Up Maine's Health Insurance Exchange," *Bangor Daily News*, November 16, 2012, http:// bangordailynews.com/2012/11/15/health/lepage-wont-lift-a-finger-to-set-up-maines-health-insurance-exchange/.

3. Robert Pear, Sharon LaFraniere, and Ian Austen, "From the Start, Signs of Trouble at Health Portal," *New York Times*, October 12, 2013, http://www.nytimes.com/2013/10/13/us/politics/from-the-start-signs-of-trouble-at-health-portal.html.

4. Amy Schatz, "Exchange Site Needs Hundreds of Fixes," *Wall Street Journal*, November 6, 2013, http://online.wsj.com/news/ articles/SB10001424052702303309504579181763508216406.

5. "Delaware Health Insurance Exchange Off to Slow Start, with Only 4 Enrollments Reported," *Washington Post*, November 6, 2013, http:// www.washingtonpost.com/national/delaware-health-insurance-exchange-off-to-slow-start-with-only-4-enrollments-reported /2013/11/06/6049003e-4728-11e3-95a9-3f15b5618ba8_story.html.

6. "Exec at HealthCare.gov Contractor Went to School with First Lady, Donated to Obama Campaign," Fox News, October 29, 2013, http://www.foxnews.com/politics/2013/10/29/healthcare-execs-obamas-political-donors/.

7. Alex Wayne and Kathleen Miller, "Obamacare Expedited Bidding Limited Who Could Build Site," Bloomberg, November 4, 2013, http://www.bloomberg.com/news/2013-11-04/obamacare-expedited-bidding-limited-who-could-build-site.html.

8.   Jayne O'Donnell and Annika McGinnis, "Big Insurers Avoid Many State Health Exchanges," *USA Today*, October 21, 2013, http://www.usatoday.com/story/news/nation/2013/10/20/little-competition-insurers-some-states-obamacare-plans/2986795/.

9.   Robb Mandelbaum, "Why Labeling Health Plans Gold, Silver or Bronze Doesn't Help," *New York Times*, October 2, 2013, http://boss.blogs.nytimes.com/2013/10/02/why-labeling-health-plans-gold-silver-or-bronze-doesnt-help/.

10.   Howard K. Koh, Garth Graham, and Sherry A. Glied, "Reducing Racial and Ethnic Disparities: The Action Plan from the Department of Health and Human Services," *Health Affairs* 30, no. 1 (October 2011).

11.   Avik Roy, "49-State Analysis: Obamacare to Increase Individual-Market Premiums by Average of 41%," *Forbes*, November 4, 2013, http://www.forbes.com/sites/theapothecary/2013/11/04/49-state-analysis-obamacare-to-increase-individual-market-premiums-by-avg-of-41-subsidies-flow-to-elderly/.

12.   Ibid.

13.   Ibid.

14.   Aaron Blake, "Obama Blames Bad Apple Insurers for Canceled Insurance Plans," *Washington Post*, October 30, 2013, http://www.washingtonpost.com/blogs/post-politics/wp/2013/10/30/obama-blames-bad-apple-insurers-for-canceled-insurance-plans/.

15.   Mary Bruce, "Obama Tweaking 'If You Like Your Plan, You Can Keep Your Plan,'" ABC News, November 4, 2013, http://abcnews.go.com/blogs/politics/2013/11/obama-tweaking-if-you-like-your-plan-you-can-keep-your-plan/.

16.   Sarah Palermo, "Concord Hospital Not Part of Provider Network for Obamacare Exchange Plan in N.H.," *Concord Monitor*, September 6, 2013, http://www.concordmonitor.com/news/8366940-95/concord-hospital-not-part-of-provider-network-for-obamacare-exchange-plan-in-nh.

17.   Watchdog.org, "Which Top Hospitals Take Your Health Insurance under Obamacare?" *U.S. News & World Report*, October 30, 2013, http://health.usnews.com/health-news/hospital-of-tomorrow/articles/2013/10/30/which-top-hospitals-take-your-health-insurance-under-obamacare.

18.   Text of the Affordable Care Act, Government Printing Office, http://www.gpo.gov/fdsys/pkg/BILLS-111hr3590enr/pdf/BILLS-111hr3590enr.pdf.

19. "Exchanges Go Live: Early Trends in Exchange Dynamics," McKinsey Center for U.S. Health System Reform, October 2013, 3.

20. "Now They Tell Us: ObamaCare Has Huge Hidden Costs," *Investor's Business Daily*, September 23, 2013, http://news.investors.com/ibd-editorials-obama-care/092313-672198-obamacare-has-huge-hidden-premium-costs-.htm.

21. Carl Campanile, "Docs Resisting ObamaCare," *New York Post*, October 29, 2013, http://nypost.com/2013/10/29/docs-resisting-obamacare/.

22. Text of the Affordable Care Act, Government Printing Office, http://www.gpo.gov/fdsys/pkg/BILLS-111hr3590enr/pdf/BILLS-111hr3590enr.pdf.

23. Roy, "49-State Analysis."

24. Transcript of U.S. Senate Finance Committee hearing, November 6, 2013, Federal News Service, available on the *National Journal* website, http://www.nationaljournal.com/free/document/4730.

25. Betsy McCaughey, "Community Organizations: Obama's Corrupt Power Grab," Human Events, June 3, 2013, http://www.humanevents.com/2013/06/03/community-organizations-obamas-corrupt-power-grab/.

26. Senator Alex Padilla's Office, "California Health Benefit Exchange to Register Voters," *Santa Clarita Valley Signal*, May 17, 2013, http://www.signalscv.com/archives/105384/.

27. Anne McLeod and Amber Kemp, "Covered California Announces $37 Million in Outreach and Education Grants," California Hospital Association, May 16, 2013, http://www.calhospital.org/covered-california-awards-grants.

28. Covered California, "Outreach and Education Grant Program—Notice of Intent to Award," May 14, 2013, http://www.healthexchange.ca.gov/Documents/COVERED%20CA%20-%20Grantee%20Profiles%20-%205-14-13.pdf.

Chapter Four: What Employers and Employees Need to Know

1. Shubham Singhal, Jeris Stueland, and Drew Ungerman, "How US Health Care Reform Will Affect Employee Benefits," McKinsey & Company, June 2011, http://www.mckinsey.com/insights/health_systems_and_services/how_us_health_care_reform_will_affect_employee_benefits.

2. Congressional Budget Office, "May 2013 Estimate of the Effects of the Affordable Care Act on Health Insurance Coverage," http://www.cbo.gov/sites/default/files/cbofiles/attachments/44190_EffectsAffordableCareActHealthInsuranceCoverage_2.pdf.

3. Barack Obama, "Remarks by the President at the Annual Conference of the American Medical Association," whitehouse.gov, June 15, 2009, http://www.whitehouse.gov/the-press-office/remarks-president-annual-conference-american-medical-association.

4. Timothy Jost, "Implementing Health Reform: Grandfathered Plans," Health Affairs (blog), June 15, 2010, http://healthaffairs.org/blog/2010/06/15/implementing-health-reform-grandfathered-plans/.

5. Steven Greenhouse, "U.P.S. to End Health Benefits for Spouses of Some Workers," *New York Times*, August 21, 2013, http://www.nytimes.com/2013/08/22/business/ups-to-end-health-benefits-for-spouses-of-some-workers.html?_r=0.

6. Chris Burritt, "Home Depot Sending 20,000 Part-Timers to Health Exchanges," Bloomberg, September 19, 2013, http://www.bloomberg.com/news/2013-09-19/home-depot-sending-20-000-part-timers-to-health-exchanges.html.

7. Avik Roy, "Delta Air Lines: Next Year, Our Health Care Costs Will Increase by 'Nearly $100 Million,'" *Forbes*, August 22, 2013, http://www.forbes.com/sites/theapothecary/2013/08/22/delta-air-lines-next-year-our-health-care-costs-will-increase-by-nearly-100-million/.

8. Janet Adamy, "McDonald's May Drop Health Plan," *Wall Street Journal*, September 30, 2010, http://online.wsj.com/news/articles/SB10001424052748703431604575522413101063070.

9. Sam Baker, "HHS Grants 106 New Healthcare Waivers," Healthwatch (The Hill's healthcare blog), August 19, 2011, http://thehill.com/blogs/healthwatch/health-reform-implementation/177581-hhs-grants-106-new-healthcare-waivers.

10. James Sherk, "Obamacare Will Price Less Skilled Workers Out of Full-Time Jobs," The Heritage Foundation Web Memo, October 11, 2011, http://www.heritage.org/research/reports/2011/10/obamacare-will-price-less-skilled-workers-out-of-full-time-jobs.

11. Dan Danner, "NFIB: Mandate Ends Vital Freedoms," *USA Today*, June 28, 2012, http://usatoday30.usatoday.com/news/opinion/editorials/story/2012-06-28/National-Federation-of-Independent-Business/55902216/1.

12. Sherk, "Obamacare Will Price Less Skilled Workers out of Full-Time Jobs."

13. "The Attack on Self-Insurance," *Wall Street Journal*, September 12, 2013, http://online.wsj.com/news/articles/SB10001424127887324886704579053042138004388.

14. Elise Viebeck, "One in 10 Employers Plans to Drop Health Benefits, Study Finds," Healthwatch (The Hill's healthcare blog), July 24, 2012, http://64.147.104.30/blogs/healthwatch/health-reform-implementation/239689-deloitte-one-in-10-employers-will-drop-health-benefits.

15. Singhal, Stueland, and Ungerman, "How US Health Care Reform Will Affect Employee Benefits."

16. Linda J. Blumberg, Matthew Buettgens, Judy Feder, and John Holahan, "Why Employers Will Continue to Provide Health Insurance: The Impact of the Affordable Care Act," Urban Institute, October 26, 2011; Lisa Dubay, John Holahan, Sharon K. Long, and Emily Lawton, "Will the Affordable Care Act Be a Job Killer?" Urban Institute, October 22, 2012.

17. Julie Jargon, "Chili's Feels Heat to Pare Costs," *Wall Street Journal*, January 28, 2011, http://online.wsj.com/news/articles/SB10001424052748704307404576080340742759346.

18. Robert J. Samuelson, "Is ObamaCare a Job Killer? Evidence Suggests Yes," *Investor's Business Daily*, October 30, 2013, http://news.investors.com/ibd-editorials-viewpoint/103013-677307-obamacare-disincentives-encourage-companies-not-to-hire.htm?ven=rss.

19. Jed Graham, "ObamaCare Pushes Low-Wage Workweek to Record Low," *Investor's Business Daily*, September 6, 2013, http://news.investors.com/politics-obamacare/090613-670104-obamacare-spurs-shortest-low-wage-week-ever.htm.

20. Betsy McCaughey, "Outlook for Workers Is Worst in Decades, Thanks to Obama," *Investor's Business Daily*, September 3, 2013, http://betsymccaughey.com/outlook-for-workers-is-worst-in-decades/.

21. Graham, "ObamaCare Pushes Low-Wage Workweek to Record Low."

22. Jed Graham, "ObamaCare Cutting Hours at Goodwill, Salvation Army?" *Investor's Business Daily*, October 4, 2013, http://news.investors.com/politics-obamacare/100413-673893-obamacare-employer-mandate-list-rises-to-319-cutting-jobs-hours.htm.

23. Andrew Puzder, "ObamaCare and the Part-Time Economy," *Wall Street Journal*, October 10, 2013, http://online.wsj.com/news/articles/SB10001424052702303382004579127162339871336.

24. Grady Payne, testimony before the Subcommittee on Health Care, Committee on Oversight and Government Reform, U.S. House of Representatives, July 28, 2011, http://www.gpo.gov/fdsys/pkg/CHRG-112hhrg71968/html/CHRG-112hhrg71968.htm.

25. Tony Pugh, "Surprise Delay in Obamacare Will Be Costly," McClatchy DC, July 3, 2013, http://www.mcclatchydc.com/2013/07/03/195756/surprise-delay-in-obamacare-will.html.

26. Paul Fronstin, "Sources of Health Insurance and Characteristics of the Uninsured: Analysis of the March 2012 Current Population Survey," Employee Benefit Research Institute Issue Brief, September 2012, http://www.ebri.org/pdf/briefspdf/EBRI_IB_09-2012_No376_Sources1.pdf.

27. Transcript of Nancy Pelosi Press Conference, October 10, 2013, available on her website, http://pelosi.house.gov/news/press-releases/transcript-of-pelosi-press-conference-today-51.

Chapter Five: Paying for More Benefits You Don't Want

1. Karen M. Beauregard, "Persons Denied Private Health Insurance due to Poor Health," Agency for Health Care Policy & Research, Report No. 92-0016, December 1991. Only adults purchasing health coverage in the individual market can be denied coverage, and that is a tiny fraction of all those covered.

2. "Coverage of Uninsurable Pre-Existing Conditions: State and Federal High Risk Pools," National Conference of State Legislatures, updated July 2013, http://www.ncsl.org/research/health/high-risk-pools-for-health-coverage.aspx.

Chapter Six: Medicaid Nation

1. Edmund F. Haislmaier and Brian Blase, "Obamacare: Impact on States," The Heritage Foundation, July 1, 2010, http://www.heritage.org/research/reports/2010/07/obamacare-impact-on-states.

2. Ibid.

3. "Obamacare's 'Baby Elephant,'" *Wall Street Journal*, February 22, 2013, http://online.wsj.com/news/articles/SB1000142412788732 3951904578288250723189588.

4. Edward Miller, "Health Reform Could Harm Medicaid Patients," *Wall Street Journal*, December 4, 2009, http://online.wsj.com/news/articles/SB10001424052748703939404574567981549184844.

5. D. J. LaPar et al., "Primary Payer Status Affects Mortality," *Annals of Internal Medicine* 252 (2010): 3; Avik Roy, "The Urgency of Medicaid Reform," The Health Care Blog, March 9, 2011, http://thehealthcareblog.com/blog/2011/03/09/the-urgency-of-medicaid-reform/.

6. Michael A. Gaglia Jr. et al., "Effect of Insurance Type on Adverse Cardiac Events after Percutaneou Coronary Intervention," *Journal of the American College of Cardiology* 107:5, 675–80. For an excellent review of studies on Medicaid outcomes, see Scott Gottlieb, "Medicaid Is Worse than No Coverage at All," *Wall Street Journal*, March 10, 2011, http://online.wsj.com/news/articles/SB1 0001424052748704758904576188280858303612.

7. The best review of these studies is Brian Blase, "Medicaid Provides Poor Quality Care: What the Research Shows," The Heritage Foundation, May 5, 2011, http://www.heritage.org/research/reports/2011/05/medicaid-provides-poor-quality-care-what-the-research-shows.

8. Paul R. Houchens, "ACA Impact on Premium Rates in the Individual and Small Group Markets," Milliman Health Care Exchange Issue Brief: Indiana Exchange Policy Committee, June 2011, http://www.in.gov/aca/files/ACAImpactonPremium Rates_v_June_2011.pdf.

9. Jeff Rhodes, "Lots of Washingtonians Want Medicaid; Few Buying Insurance," The Olympia Report, October 30, 2013, http://theolympiareport.com/far-more-washingtonians-applying-for-medicaid-than-buying-inurance/.

10. Amy Schatz and Jennifer Corbett Dooren, "States Report Medicaid Surge after Health-Law Roll Out," *Wall Street Journal*, October 28, 2013, http://stream.wsj.com/story/latest-headlines/SS-2-63399/SS-2-365556/?cid=xrs_rss-nd%3C.

11. Sean P. Keehan et al., "National Health Spending Projections," *Health Affairs* 31, no. 7 (July 2012): 1600–10.

Chapter Seven: Obamacare Raids Medicare and Hurts Seniors

1. Andrea M. Sisko et al., "National Health Spending Projections," *Health Affairs* 29, no. 10 (October 2010): 1933–41.
2. Richard S. Foster, "The Financial Outlook for Medicare," testimony before the House Committee on the Budget, July 13, 2011; Kaiser Health News, July 14, 2011.
3. Vivan Wu and Yu-Chu Shen, "The Long Term Impact of Medicare Payment Reductions on Patient Outcomes," National Bureau of Economic Research, working paper no. 16859, March 2011.
4. Peter Orszag, "Health Costs Are the Real Deficit Threat: That's Why President Obama Is Making Health-Care Reform a Priority," *Wall Street Journal*, May 15, 2009, http://online.wsj.com/news/articles/SB124234365947221489; Dartmouth Atlas White Paper, December 2008.
5. John E. Wennberg et al., "Improving Quality and Curbing Health Care Spending," *Dartmouth Atlas of Health Care 2008.*
6. John A. Romley et al., "Hospital Spending and Inpatient Mortality," *Archives of Internal Medicine* 154:3 (February 1, 2011).
7. President Barack Obama, "Remarks by the President in ABC 'Prescription for America' Town Hall on Health Care," White House Office of the Press Secretary, June 25, 2009.
8. Peter Cram et al., "Total Knee Arthroplasty Volume, Utilization, and Outcomes among Medicare Beneficiaries, 1991–2012," *Journal of the American Medical Association* 308:12 (September 26, 2012).
9. Dr. Seymour Cohen, statement at the October 19, 2009, forum at the Grand Hyatt Hotel, New York City.
10. Stephen Nohlgren "Patients Scramble after AARP Medicare Advantage Plans Drop Providers," *Tampa Bay Times*, October 21, 2013, http://www.tampabay.com/news/health/patients-scramble-after-aarp-medicare-advantage-plans-drop-providers/2148424.

11. Felice J. Freyer "UnitedHealthcare Dropping R.I. Doctors from Medicare Advantage Network/Poll," *Providence Journal*, October 21, 2013, http://www.providencejournal.com/breaking-news/content/20131021-unitedhealthcare-dropping-r.i.-doctors-from-medicare-advantage-network-poll.ece.

12. Carl Campanile "Elderly Patients Sick over Losing Doctors under Obamacare," *New York Post*, October 25, 2013, http://nypost.com/2013/10/25/elderly-patients-sick-over-losing-doctors-under-obamacare/.

13. "Comparison of Projected Enrollment in Medicare Advantage Plans and Subsidies for Extra Benefits Not Covered by Medicare under Current Law and under Reconciliation Legislation Combined with H.R. 3590 as Passed by the Senate," Congressional Budget Office, March 19, 2010. See also Richard S. Foster, "Estimated Financial Effects of the 'Patient Protection and Affordable Care Act' as Amended," Centers for Medicare and Medicaid Services, April 22, 2010, http://www.cms.gov/Research-Statistics-Data-and-Systems/Research/ActuarialStudies/downloads/PPACA_2010-04-22.pdf.

14. "Text: Obama's AMA Speech on Health Care," CBSNews.com, June 15, 2009.

15. Howard Dean, "The Affordable Care Act's Rate-Setting Won't Work," *Wall Street Journal*, July 28, 2013, http://online.wsj.com/news/articles/SB10001424127887324110404578628542498014414.

16. Foster, "Estimated Financial Effects."

17. Ibid. Closing the donut hole will cost $12 billion from 2010 through 2019.

Chapter Eight: The Tax Man Cometh

1. J. Russell George, press release, "The IRS Has Made Significant Progress in Planning for the Implementation of the Affordable Care Act," October 24, 2011.

2. J. Russell George, memorandum for Secretary Geithner, "Management and Performance Challenges Facing the Internal Revenue Service for Fiscal Year 2012," 12.

3. Joint Committee on Taxation, estimate updated as of July 2012, reported by William McBride, "Obamacare Taxes Now Estimated to Cost $1 Trillion over 10 Years," Tax Foundation, July 25, 2012.

4. Congressional Budget Office, letter to the Honorable Evan Bayh, November 30, 2009; Joint Committee on Taxation, letter to the Honorable Jon Kyl, May 12, 2011.

5. Congressional Budget Office, "Estimates for the Insurance Coverage Provisions of the Affordable Care Act Updated for the Recent Supreme Court Decision," July 23, 2012, table 4. (The employer mandate was projected to yield $117 billion and the individual mandate penalty to yield $55 billion.)

6. Center for Health Policy Studies and Vivek Rajasekhar, "Implementation of the Major Provisions of Obamacare: The Timeline," The Heritage Foundation, http://blog.heritage.org/wp-content/uploads/timeline_chart4-8final.pdf; and Chris Conover, "Why Conservatives Shouldn't Cheer the Cadillac Tax (and Neither Should Anyone Else)," *Forbes*, June 5, 2013, http://www.forbes.com/sites/theapothecary/2013/06/05/why-conservatives-shouldnt-cheer-the-cadillac-tax-and-neither-should-anyone-else/.

7. Congressional Budget Office, letter to the Honorable John Boehner, July 23, 2012.

8. Ricardo Alonso-Zaldivar and Andrew Taylor, "Budget Office: Obama's Health Law Reduces Deficit," *Denver Post*, July 24, 2012, http://www.denverpost.com/breakingnews/ci_21146746/budget-office-obamas-health-law-reduces-deficit.

9. CMS National Health Expenditure Projections 2012–2022, Centers for Medicare & Medicaid Services, http://www.cms.gov/Research-Statistics-Data-and-Systems/Statistics-Trends-and-Reports/NationalHealthExpendData/Downloads/Proj2012.pdf.

10. Ibid.

11. "Hoyer: New CBO Report Confirms Health Care Law Controls Costs, Reduces Deficit," Steny Hoyer press release, July 24, 2012, http://www.democraticwhip.gov/content/hoyer-new-cbo-report-confirms-health-care-law-controls-costs-reduces-deficit.

12. CMS National Health Expenditure Projections 2012–2022.

Chapter Nine: Doctors Reject Obamacare

1. Emily P. Walker, "AMA Makes Small Gain in Membership," MedPage Today, June 17, 2012, http://www.medpagetoday.com/MeetingCoverage/AMA/33320.

2.   Parija Kavilanz, "Doctors Going Broke," CNN, January 6, 2012, http://money.cnn.com/2012/01/05/smallbusiness/doctors_broke/.

3.   Marc Siegel, "Will Your Doctor Quit? Obamacare Foretells Mass Exodus from Patient Care," *Forbes*, August 12, 2012, http://www.forbes.com/sites/marcsiegel/2012/08/12/will-your-doctor-quit-obamacare-foretells-mass-exodus-from-patient-care/.

4.   Hal Scherz, "Doctors Drowning in Alphabet Soup," Townhall.com, March 8, 2011, http://finance.townhall.com/columnists/halscherz/2011/03/08/doctors_drowning_in_alphabet_soup/page/full.

5.   David Blumenthal, "Stimulating the Adoption of Health Information Technology," *New England Journal of Medicine*, April 9, 2009, http://www.nejm.org/doi/full/10.1056/NEJMp0901592.

6.   Michelle Malkin, "O'Care's Other Horror," *New York Post*, October 23, 2013.

7.   Bradley Allen, "ObamaCare 2016: Happy Yet?" *Wall Street Journal*, October 22, 2013, http://online.wsj.com/news/articles/SB10001424052702303448104579149642030106.

8.   "2013 Deloitte Survey of U.S. Physicians," Deloitte Center for Health Solutions, http://www.deloitte.com/view/en_US/us/Insights/centers/center-for-health-solutions/a5ee019120e6d310VgnVCM1000003256f70aRCRD.htm.

Chapter Ten:
Obamacare vs. the Rule of Law

1.   Mary Lu Carnevale, "Obama to GOP: 'I Won,'" *Wall Street Journal*, January 23, 2009, http://blogs.wsj.com/washwire/2009/01/23/obama-to-gop-i-won/.

2.   Jonathan Weisman and Robert Pear, "Seeing Opening, House G.O.P. Pushes Delay on Individual Mandate in Health Law," *New York Times*, July 9, 2013, http://www.nytimes.com/2013/07/10/us/politics/house-gop-pushes-delay-on-individual-mandate-in-health-law.html?_r=0.

3.   The two cases are Train v. City of New York, 420 U.S. 35 (1975) and Clinton v. City of New York, 524 U.S. 417 (1998).

4.   "A Senate Divided: GOP Senator Says Mike Lee's Plan to Defund Obamacare Is the 'Dumbest Idea I've Ever Heard,'" The Blaze,

July 25, 2013, http://www.theblaze.com/stories/2013/07/25/a-senate-divided-gop-senator-says-mike-lees-plan-to-defund-obamacare-is-the-dumbest-idea-ive-ever-heard/.

5. Ibid.

6. "JW Files Suit on behalf of Kawa Orthodontics against Treasury & IRS to Overturn Delay of Obamacare Employer Mandate," Judicial Watch press release, October 1, 2013, http://www.judicialwatch.org/press-room/press-releases/judicial-watch-files-suit-on-behalf-of-dr-larry-kawa-of-kawa-orthodontics-against-obama-treasury-irs-to-overturn-delay-of-obamacare-employer-mandate/.

7. In re: Aiken County et al., Case No. 11-1271 (D.C. Cir. Aug. 13, 2013) http://www.cadc.uscourts.gov/internet/opinions.nsf/BAE0CF34F762EBD985257BC6004DEB18/$file/11-1271-1451347.pdf.

8. George Bennett, "Boca Raton Dentist Sues over Obama's Delay of Employer Mandate under Health-Care Law," *Palm Beach Post*, October 1, 2013, http://www.palmbeachpost.com/news/news/local/boca-dentist-sues-over-obamas-delay-of-employer-ma/nbCk8/.

9. Michael Patrick Leahy, "Justice Roberts Turns Obamacare into Origination Clause Shell Game," Breitbart.com, July 1, 2012, http://www.breitbart.com/Big-Government/2012/06/29/Justice-Roberts.

10. James Madison, *The Federalist* No. 48, "These Departments Should Not Be So Far Separated as to Have No Constitutional Control over Each Other," from the New York Packet, Friday, February 1, 1788, Yale Law School's Avalon Project, http://avalon.law.yale.edu/18th_century/fed48.asp.

11. Gonzales v. Oregon, 546 U.S. 243 (2006).

12. "Judge: Late-Term Abortion Ban Unconstitutional," CNN, August 26, 2004, http://www.cnn.com/2004/LAW/08/26/abortion/.

13. Coons v. Geithner, No. 2-10-cv-01714-ECV, complaint filed in the District Court of Arizona on August 12, 2010.

14. Diane Cohen and Michael F. Cannon, "The Independent Payment Advisory Board: PPACA's Anti-Constitutional and Authoritarian Super-Legislature," CATO Institute Policy Analysis No. 700, June 14, 2012, http://www.cato.org/publications/policy-analysis/independent-payment-advisory-board-ppacas-anticonstitutional-authoritarian-superlegislature.

Chapter Eleven: If You Like Your God, You Can Keep Your God

1. Sarah Wheaton, "Court Rules Contraception Mandate Infringes on Religious Freedom," *New York Times*, November 1, 2013, http://www.nytimes.com/2013/11/02/us/court-rules-contraception-mandate-infringes-on-religious-freedom.html.

2. Dave Larsen, "Sidney Companies' Lawsuit Challenges Federal Contraception Mandate," *Journal-News*, January 25, 2013, http://www.journal-news.com/news/business/sidney-companies-lawsuit-challenges-federal-contra/nT6zK/.

3. Francis A. Gilardi, et al. v. United States Department of Health and Human Services, et al., Circuit docket 13-5069 (D.C. Cir. 2013), citing James 2:26 (King James Version), http://www.gpo.gov/fdsys/pkg/USCOURTS-caDC-13-05069/pdf/USCOURTS-caDC-13-05069-0.pdf.

4. Larsen, "Sidney Companies' Lawsuit Challenges Federal Contraception Mandate."

5. Sherbert v. Verner, 374 U.S. 398 (1963), at 402.

6. Text of the Religious Freedom Restoration Act of 1993 available online at the Department of Justice website, http://www.justice.gov/jmd/ls/legislative_histories/pl103-141/act-pl103-141.pdf; David M. Ackerman, "The Religious Freedom Restoration Act and the Religious Freedom Act: A Legal Analysis," Congressional Research Service Report for Congress, April 17, 1992, http://www.justice.gov/jmd/ls/legislative_histories/pl103-141/crsrept-1992.pdf.

7. For updates, see the Becket Fund for Religious Liberty's HHS Mandate Information Central, http://www.becketfund.org/hhsinformationcentral/.

8. See the Becket Fund for Religious Liberty's case page on *Hobby Lobby v. Sebelius*, http://www.becketfund.org/hobbylobby/.

9. "Contraception Coverage: A Hobby Shop Is Not a Church," *Los Angeles Times*, September 24, 2013, http://www.latimes.com/opinion/editorials/la-ed-contraceptives-20130924,0,84089.story#axzz2jhAyoFrP.

10. "Birth Control and a Boss's Religious Views," *New York Times*, September 29, 2013, http://www.nytimes.com/2013/09/30/opinion/birth-control-and-a-bosss-religious-views.html.

11. Francis A. Gilardi, et al. v. United States Department of Health and Human Services, et al., Circuit docket 13-5069 (D.C. Cir. 2013).

12. James Taranto, "When the Archbishop Met the President," *Wall Street Journal*, March 31, 2012, http://online.wsj.com/news/articles/SB10001424052702303816504577311800821270184.

13. "Religious Sisters File First Class-Action Lawsuit against Controversial HHS Mandate," Becket Fund for Religious Liberty, September 24, 2013, http://www.becketfund.org/religious-sisters-file-first-class-action-lawsuit-against-controversial-hhs-mandate/.

14. "Plaintiffs' Memorandum of Law Pursuant to Court's July 25, 2013 Scheduling Order," Archdiocese of New York v. Sebelius, filed September 26, 2013, Eastern District of New York.

15. Ibid.

Chapter Twelve: Washington's Misguided Views on Health Reform

1. Sean P. Keehan et al., "National Health Spending Projections," *Health Affairs* 31, no. 7 (July 2012): 1600–10.

2. Tarren Bragdon, "Rx NY: A Prescription for More Accessible Health Care in NY," Empire Center for New York State Policy, December 11, 2007.

3. Nancy-Ann DeParle, "One Year of the Affordable Care Act," White House Blog, March 23, 2009.

4. Robert Steinbrook, "Saying No Isn't NICE: The Travails of Britain's National Institute for Health and Clinical Excellence," *New England Journal of Medicine*, 359 (November 6, 2008): 1977–81.

5. Mark W. Stanton, "The High Concentration of U.S. Health Care Expenditures," Agency for Healthcare Research and Quality, Research in Action, issue 19, June 2006.

6. Ezekiel Emanuel and Victor Fuchs, "The Perfect Storm of Overutilization," *Journal of the American Medical Association* 299, no. 23 (June 18, 2008): 2789–91.

7.   Congressional Budget Office, "Key Issues in Analyzing Major Health Insurance Proposals," December 18, 2008, publication 41746; Congressional Budget Office, "Technological Change and the Growth of Health Care Spending," January 31, 2008.

8.   David Cutler and Mark McClellan, "Is Technological Change in Medicine Worth It?" *Health Affairs* 20, no. 5 (September 2001): 11–29.

9.   Kathleen Sebelius, "Sebelius Statement on New Medicare Trustees Report," press release, U.S. Department of Health and Human Services, May 12, 2009.

10.   Council of Economic Advisors, "The Economic Case for Health Care Reform," released June 2, 2009, published by the White House.

11.   U. W. Reinhart et al., "US Health in an International Context," *Health Affairs* 23, no. 3 (March 2004): 10–25.

12.   David Blumenthal, "Controlling Health Care Expenditures," *New England Journal of Medicine* 344 (March 8, 2001): 766–69.

13.   Transcript of *Meet the Press*, Tom Daschle guest, August 16, 2009, available at www.msnbc.msn.com.

14.   Transcript of *Larry King Live*, CNN, August 12, 2009.

15.   The *Tampa Bay Times* operates a website called PolitiFact. Even now it repeats the WHO 37th-place ranking and uses it to rebut the claims that the U.S. has superior healthcare. For example, it cited the now twelve-year-old WHO report on July 9, 2012, to rebut Speaker of the House John Boehner and again on August 30, 2012, to refute New Jersey Governor Chris Christie's statement that healthcare is best in the U.S.

16.   World Health Organization, "The World Health Report 2000."

17.   Letter of Philip Musgrove to the *New England Journal of Medicine* 362 (April 22, 2010): 1546–47.

18.   Francis Berrno et al., "Survival for Eight Major Cancers and All Cancers Combined for European Adults Diagnosed in 1995–99: Results of the EUROCARE-4 Study," *Lancet Oncology* 8, no. 9 (September 2007): 773–83.

Chapter Thirteen: Beating Obamacare

1.   See, for example, "55% Favor Repeal of Obamacare," Rasmussen Reports, November 12, 2012, http://www.rasmussenreports.

com/public_content/politics/general_politics/november_
2013/55_favor_repeal_of_obamacare.

2.   Robert Pear, "Notes Reveal Chaotic White House Talks on Health
      Care Site," *New York Times*, November 5, 2013, http://www.
      nytimes.com/2013/11/06/us/politics/senator-cites-crisis-of-
      confidence-on-health-care-site.html?_r=1&.

3.   "RNC Chair: 'We Will Tattoo' Obamacare to Dems' Foreheads
      in 2014 Elections," CBS, November 11, 2013, http://washington.
      cbslocal.com/2013/11/11/rnc-chair-we-will-tattoo-obamacare-
      to-dems-foreheads-in-2014-elections/.

4.   See Section 1312(d)(3)(D) of the Affordable Care Act, Govern-
      ment Printing Office, http://www.gpo.gov/fdsys/pkg/BILLS-
      111hr3590enr/pdf/BILLS-111hr3590enr.pdf.

5.   See Uwe E. Reinhardt, "A Health Care Fight That Punishes Federal
      Workers," *New York Times*, September 27, 2013, http://economix.
      blogs.nytimes.com/2013/09/27/a-health-care-fight-that-
      punishes-federal-workers/.

6.   See Paul Gigot, "Congress's ObamaCare Exemption," *Wall Street
      Journal*, August 5, 2013, http://online.wsj.com/news/articles/SB1
      0001424127887324635904578644202946287548.

7.   Information via ehealthinsurance.com.

Who Gains and Who Loses

1.   Fred Lucas, "Obama Cabinet Secretary: 'The Private Market Is
      in a Death Spiral,'" CNSNews, February 29, 2012, http://cnsnews.
      com/news/article/obama-cabinet-secretary-private-market-
      death-spiral.

2.   Goldwater Institute lawsuit challenging the Patient Protection
      and Affordable Care Act.

The Obamacare Dictionary

1.   Bill Keller, "Obamacare: The Rest of the Story," *New York Times*,
      October 13, 2013, http://www.nytimes.com/2013/10/14/opinion/
      keller-obamacare-the-rest-of-the-story.html.

2.   See the U.S. Department of Labor's Technical Release 2012-01,
      "Frequently Asked Questions from Employers Regarding

Automatic Enrollment, Employer Shared Responsibility, and Waiting Periods," February 9, 2012, http://www.dol.gov/ebsa/newsroom/tr12-01.html.

3. See "Excise Tax on 'Cadillac' Plans," Health Policy Briefs, Health Affairs website, September 12, 2013, http://www.healthaffairs.org/healthpolicybriefs/brief.php?brief_id=99.

4. Howard K. Koh, Garth Graham, and Sherry A. Glied, "Reducing Racial and Ethnic Disparities: The Action Plan from the Department of Health and Human Services, *Health Affairs* 30, no. 10 (October 2011). The authors call for increased taxpayer funding to meet the needs of undocumented immigrants at the community health centers.

5. See the Centers for Disease Control and Prevention (CDC) factsheet, "Community Transformation Grants Program," http://www.cdc.gov/communitytransformation/pdf/ctg-factsheet.pdf.

6. Community Transformation Grant (CTG) Program Fact Sheet, Centers for Disease Control and Prevention, http://www.cdc.gov/communitytransformation/funds/index.htm. All other information about Community Health Councils was found on the organization's own website at www.chc-inc.org.

7. For the administration's statements that the loans will not be repaid, see "Healthwatch," The Hill, July 18, 2011. For an updated list of recipients, see the HHS website. For a sample of press coverage on the loans, see Andrea K. Walker, "U.S. Loan to Kick-Start Md. Insurance Co-op," *Baltimore Sun*, September 29, 2012; "CMS Awards Two Co-op Loans," American Hospital Association press release, September 4, 2012; "Western States Lead the Way on Healthcare COOP Development," *Business Wire*, August 8, 2012; Senator Michael F. Bennet (Democrat, Colorado) press release, "Bennet Applauds Announcement of $69 Million Loan for Colorado Health Insurance Cooperative," July 27, 2012.

8. Jerry Markon, "Health Co-ops, Created to Foster Competition and Lower Insurance Costs, Are in Danger," *Washington Post*, October 22, 2013, http://www.washingtonpost.com/politics/health-co-ops-

created-to-foster-competition-and-lower-insurance-costs-are-facing-danger/2013/10/22/e1c961fe-3809-11e3-ae46-e4248e75c8ea_story.html.

9. Jordan Fabian, "Obama Healthcare Plan Nixes Ben Nelson's Cornhusker Kickback Deal," The Hill, February 22, 2010; Reuters, "Obama Plan Kills Cornhusker Kickback, Boosts Medicaid," February 22, 2010.

10. Koh, Graham, and Glied, "Reducing Racial and Ethnic Disparities."

11. "Health Bills in Congress Won't Fix Doctor Shortage," Kaiser Health News, October 12, 2009, http://www.kaiserhealthnews. org/stories/2009/october/12/primary-care-doctor-shortage. aspx.

12. Sally Pipes, "Thanks to Obamacare, a 20,000 Doctor Shortage Is Set to Quintuple," *Forbes*, June 10, 2013, http://www.forbes.com/ sites/sallypipes/2013/06/10/thanks-to-obamacare-a-20000-doctor-shortage-is-set-to-quintuple/.

13. See the chart provided in Joe Palazzolo, "Health Law Faces New Legal Challenges," *Wall Street Journal*, October 21, 2013, also online at "Find Your State's Health-Care Exchange," wsj.com, http://online.wsj.com/news/articles/SB10001424052702304526 204579099422440044100.

14. See "How Do I Get an Exemption from the Fee for Not Having Health Coverage?" Healthcare.gov, https://www.healthcare.gov/ exemptions/.

15. See Kyle Cheney, "Exemptions Pose Another Big Hurdle for Obamacare," Politico, October 15, 2013, http://www.politico. com/story/2013/10/obamacare-exemptions-individual-mandate-98297.html.

16. "Reports Raise Concern about Backgrounds of ObamaCare 'Navigators,'" Fox News, October 18, 2013, http://www.foxnews. com/politics/2013/10/18/reports-raise-concern-about-backgrounds-obamacare-navigators/.

17. Philip Klein, "New Menu Regulations Eat into Profits for Small Businesses," *Washington Examiner*, August 10, 2011, http://www. sfexaminer.com/sanfrancisco/new-menu-regulations-eat-into-profits-for-small-businesses/Content?oid=2179379.

18. "Obamacare's Menu Labeling Law: The Food Police Are Coming," The Heritage Foundation Issue Brief, August 6, 2013, http://www.heritage.org/research/reports/2013/08/obamacare-s-menu-labeling-law-the-food-police-are-coming.

19. "Young Adult Coverage," U.S. Department of Health and Human Services website, http://www.hhs.gov/healthcare/rights/youngadults/.

20. Koh, Graham, and Glied, "Reducing Racial and Ethnic Disparities."

21. "Affordable Care Act's Reinsurance Fee Hits Employer Plans Beginning in 2014," Aon Legislative Update, http://www.aon.com/human-capital-consulting/thought-leadership/leg_updates/healthcare/reports-pubs_ACA_Reinsurance_Fees_Hits_Employers_2014.jsp.

22. Jay Hancock, "Labor Might Have Just Gotten a Pass on an Obamacare Fee," *Washington Post*, November 6, 2013, http://www.washingtonpost.com/blogs/wonkblog/wp/2013/11/06/labor-might-have-just-gotten-a-pass-on-an-obamacare-fee/.

23. Congressional Research Service, December 10, 2010.

24. See eligibility information at the IRS website, "Small Business Health Care Tax Credit for Small Employers," http://www.irs.gov/uac/Small-Business-Health-Care-Tax-Credit-for-Small-Employers.

25. Sally Pipes, "Small-Business Health Care Tax Credits Are Having a Minuscule Impact," *Forbes*, July 4, 2011.

26. See Emily Maltby, "Health-Care Tax Credit Eludes Some," *Wall Street Journal*, June 21, 2012, http://online.wsj.com/news/articles/SB10001424052702303379204577477160299914638.

27. Tami Luhby, "What You'll Actually Pay for Obamacare," CNN, August 21, 2013, http://money.cnn.com/2013/08/21/news/economy/obamacare-subsidies/.

28. See "Income, Poverty and Health Insurance Coverage in the United States: 2012," U.S. Census news release, September 17, 2013, http://www.census.gov/newsroom/releases/archives/income_wealth/cb13-165.html.

29.   Patrick C. Walsh, "Response to the United States Preventive Services Task Force (USPSTF) Recommendation against PSA Testing for the Early Diagnosis of Prostate Cancer in Healthy Men," James Buchanan Brady Urological Institute, Johns Hopkins Medicine, no date, http://www.urology.jhu.edu/PSA_controversy.php.

30.   See the Congressional Budget Office's November 2013 report "Options for Reducing the Deficit, 2014–2023," for instance.

INDEX

2012 election, 169

A
AARP, 82, 84
abortifacients, 154. *See also*
    "morning after" drugs; Plan
    B pills
abortion, 119, 124, 129, 163–64,
    177
Accountable Care Organizations
    (ACOs), 164
Action Plan, 171–72
actuaries, 23, 69, 72, 74, 83, 133,
    160
adjusted gross income, 179–80
Administrative Procedures Act,
    112
Aetna, 4, 102
Affordable Care Act. *See also*
    Obama health law; Patient
    Protection and Affordable
    Care Act
    American Medical Association
        and, 98
    birth control and, 127, 170
    changes to, 105–7, 111, 116, 156
    Congress and, 58

costs of, 31, 94–95
    exchanges and, 113–15
    Healthcare.gov and, 9
    health insurance and, 45, 144
    IRS and, 19
    Kathleen Sebelius and, 27
    Medicaid and, 3, 72
    W-2s and, 5
    waivers and, 10
"Affordable Care Act Tool Kit,"
    37
"affordable" coverage, 31, 50, 90
Allen, Bradley, 103
American Cancer Society, 106,
    166
American Health Benefit
    Exchange, 26, 175. *See also*
    exchanges
American Indians, 18, 165, 175
American Medical Association
    (AMA), 98, 151
American Recovery and
    Reinvestment Act, 20, 100,
    109, 149, 187. *See also* stimulus
    legislation
angioplasty, 70, 78
Annals of Internal Medicine, 70

Anthem, 28, 33
Archdiocese of New York, 130
Archives of Internal Medicine, 77
Arkansas, 32
armed services, 18
assets, 66
assisted suicide, 118
"assisters," 36, 39
Associated Press, 27
Association of American Medical
    Colleges, 172
Authority for Mandate Delay
    Act, 109
automated teller machines and
    check-outs, 53
automatic enrollment, 165

B
baby boomers, 4, 68, 74, 162
Balanced Budget Act, 76
Becket Fund for Religious
    Liberty, 129
benefits, 20, 47, 50, 60–61, 66, 72,
    81, 83–84, 156, 178–79, 191
Bill of Rights, 124
birth control, 123–24,
    127–28, 130, 154. *See also*
    contraception
Blue Cross Blue Shield, 28, 33–34
Blumenthal, David, 101, 138
Boehner, John, 111
bonds, 5, 89
Bragdon, Tarren, 134
Breast Cancer in Young Women
    Initiative, 165
Brennan, William, 125
British National Health Service,
    135
Brown, Janice Rogers, 125
Budget Control Act, 95
bureaucrats, 6, 43, 84, 98, 101,
    160, 177
Bureau of Labor Statistics, 54
Burr, Richard, 112

Bush, George H. W., 109
Bush, George W., 109, 118
businesses, 5, 44, 49, 56, 69, 90,
    186–87
bypass surgery, 78

C
"Cadillac tax." *See* taxes,
    "Cadillac tax"
Caesarean section, 35
California, 28, 34, 37–40, 58, 66,
    72, 77, 99, 148, 167, 170
California NAACP, 38
Campregon, Jeannette, 82–83
cancellations, 2, 14–16, 25, 189
cancer, 82, 106, 134–35, 139–40,
    165–66, 189–90
capital gains taxes, 5, 89, 161, 180
caps, 10, 149, 178, 183
    annual, 60, 165, 191
    lifetime, 161, 191
cardiologists, 4, 35, 70
catastrophic insurance plans,
    19, 32
Catholics, 124, 136, 129–30, 191
Cedars-Sinai hospital, 3, 33, 99
Centers for Disease Control and
    Prevention (CDC), 165, 167
Centers for Medicare & Medicaid
    Services (CMS), 94, 133, 166
CGI Federal, 28
Children's Health Insurance
    Program (CHIP), 66, 178
Children's Heart Institute, 103
Chili's Grill and Bar, 52
Christians, 124, 128, 177
chronically ill patients, 161
Chu, Stephen, 114
Cigna, 4, 102
CKE Restaurants, 54
Clinton, Bill, 109
CNN, 98, 138, 143
Cohen, Diane, 120
Cohen, Seymour, 80

Colorado, 32
community health centers, 164, 166–67, 180
Community Health Councils, 39, 167–68
community organizers, 38
community transformation grants, 160, 167
Comparative Effectiveness Research, 168
concierge medicine, 102–3
Congress, 9, 55, 101, 107, 138, 141, 154
    Affordable Care Act and, 58, 147
    American Recovery and Reinvestment Act and, 187
    Barack Obama and, 44, 62, 105, 108–9, 112, 114, 117
    "Cadillac" tax and 93
    Children's Health Insurance Program and, 178
    Constitution and, 112, 116, 121, 144
    contraception and, 127
    deadlines from, 10
    Independent Payment Advisory Board and, 84–85, 120, 177
    James Madison and, 11, 110, 112
    Kathleen Sebelius and, 27
    Medicare and, 177, 179
    Obamacare and, 61–62, 106, 111, 141, 145, 190
    Richard S. Foster and, 76, 79
    stimulus law and, 168
Congressional Budget Office (CBO), 2, 43, 62, 90, 92–95, 136
Connecticut, 4
Consolidated Omnibus Budget Reconciliation Act (COBRA), 149–50
Consumer Operated and Oriented Plans (CO-OPS), 169

consumer protections, 60, 147–48
contraception, 123–24, 170, 174, 191. *See also* birth control
contraception mandate, 123, 191
co-pays, 17, 25, 29, 60, 153
cornhusker kickback, 170
Cornyn, John, 37
Costa Rica, 138
Council of Economic Advisors, 137
Covenant of Liberty, 116
Covered California, 28, 38
Cultural Competency Training, 171
Curley, James, 39

D
Danner, Dan, 49
Dartmouth Atlas of Health Care 2008, 77
Daschle, Tom, 138
D.C. Circuit Court of Appeals, 114
Dean, Howard, 84
Death with Dignity Act, 118
deductibles, 17, 25, 29–31, 36, 60, 115, 176–77, 184
Delaware, 27
Deloitte Consulting, 52, 97, 103
Delta Air Lines, 45
Democrats, Democratic Party, 37, 39–40, 68, 95, 109–10, 144, 149, 152, 170
demonstration projects, 171
DeParle, Nancy-Ann, 134–35
Department of Health and Human Services, 4, 15, 21, 35, 46, 63, 80, 97, 102, 127, 136, 160–76, 182, 185, 189
Department of Labor, 15, 53, 173
dependents, 17, 49, 56–57, 171
Detoy, Steven, 82
diagnostic equipment, 161

dialysis, 165
dialysis centers, 74–75, 161
disparities, 167, 171, 176
Docs4PatientCare, 99
doctors, 1, 6, 21, 74, 99, 118–19,
  160, 178
  American Medical Association
  (AMA) and, 97–98
  government control of, 97, 102–
  3, 120, 147, 162, 168, 172
  Medicaid and, 34, 69, 71–72,
  77, 79
  preferred hospitals and, 3–4, 20,
  33–35
  shortage of, 82, 172
  technology and, 100–1, 187
  treating seniors and, 75, 79, 82,
  164, 179
Dolan, Timothy, 129
Domino's Pizza, 181
Donut Hole, 85–86, 153, 172
dual eligibles, 173

E
Edwards, Harry T., 127
Eisenhower, Dwight D., 109
Ella pills, 126
Elmendorf, Douglas, 85
Emanuel, Ezekiel, 135
Emblem Health, 82
emergency care, 173
Emergency Medicaid, 173
Emergency Medical Treatment
  and Active Labor Act, 173
Empire Center for Policy
  Research, 134
employer mandate, 5, 10, 41,
  43–44, 47–58, 69, 106–14, 123,
  155–56, 173, 183, 191
employers, 2–10, 14, 26, 30–31,
  42, 49–63, 88, 92, 106–15, 123,
  126, 155–56, 171, 184–91
  fines and, 8, 53, 128–29, 183
  large employers, 8, 10, 45, 50,
  106

number of employees and, 41,
  48, 69, 90, 128, 173
  regulations and, 16, 45
  required insurance coverage
  and, 8, 165
  waivers and, 10, 46–47, 56–57,
  61, 128, 142, 153, 170, 191
Enroll America, 174, 181
entitlements, 21–23, 65, 75, 85,
  93–95, 99, 137, 146, 149
entry-level workers, 61, 69
"essential benefits," 16–17, 25, 29,
  35, 47, 50–51, 62, 84, 156, 170,
  174, 189, 192
"essential coverage," 2, 16, 18, 33,
  47, 173
Europe, 137–38, 140
exchanges, 2, 22, 26–27, 30, 33,
  35–36, 57, 62, 108, 113–14,
  155–56, 159, 171, 174–75, 180,
  183, 188–89. *See also* American
  Health Benefit Exchange
  Bronze plan, 17, 25, 29, 31, 34
  Gold plan, 17, 25, 29, 34
  health, 29, 37, 56, 72, 99, 107, 190
  Platinum plan, 17, 25, 29, 34
  Silver plan, 17, 25, 29, 31, 34
executive orders, 163–64

F
Fair Labor Standards Act, 184
Families in Good Health, 168
family coverage, 49–50, 166, 186
Federal Coordinating Council
  for Comparative Effectiveness
  Research, 168
Federal Data Hub, 175
Federal Employees Health
  Benefit Program, 144
Federalist, The, 11, 110, 118, 145
federal workers, 6
Feldt, Gloria, 119
financial hardship, 19
fines, 8, 17, 47–49, 52–53, 56–57,
  173. *See also* penalties

First Amendment, 124, 177
Fitton, Thomas, 112, 114
Flexible Savings Accounts (FSA), 87, 91
Florida, 67, 82, 105, 112
Forbes Magazine, 187
Foster, Richard S., 76, 85, 161
freedom of religion, 124, 126, 130
Free Enterprise Fund v. Public Company Accounting Oversight Board, 120
Friedman, Paul, 113
full-time employment, 47, 53–57, 107, 165, 173

G
Galloway-Gilliam, Lark, 167
generous health plans, 87, 157, 161
Geneva College, 127–28
George, J. Russell, 87
Georgia, 32, 55
Gilardi brothers, the, 124–25, 127
Goldwater Institute, 119–20
Gonzalez v. Oregon, 118
Goodwill Industries, 54
government dependency, 23
government employees, 37–38, 160
grandfather clause, the, 14–15, 159
Grant, Ulysses S., 114
Green, David, 126
gross domestic product (GDP), 94, 133
gross income, 48, 179–80

H
Hardee's, 54
Harkin, Tom, 109–10
healthcare administration, 6, 160
healthcare consumption, 4, 138
Healthcare.gov website, 9, 26, 28, 155, 175
healthcare providers, 4, 102, 164
healthcare "quality," 102, 138, 171

healthcare spending, 23, 68, 94–95, 131–33, 138, 146
Health Disparities Data Collection, 176
health reform, 2, 51, 90, 131–32, 138, 147, 151, 170
Health Savings Accounts (HSAs), 91, 176–77
heart attacks, 4, 70, 76, 136
heart disease, 7, 136
Heritage Foundation, The, 47, 50
high-deductible plans, 184
high earners, 88–90, 180
high-risk pools, 63–64, 149. *See also* temporary high-risk pool
HMO plans, 148
Hobby Lobby, 126, 154, 177
Home Depot, 45
homes, 89
hospice care, 74–75, 83, 179
hospitals, 101, 123, 136–37, 167, 173, 187
    budget cuts in, 161
    doctors and, 3–4, 20, 33–35
    in Florida, 82
    Independent Payment Advisory Board and, 83–84, 177
    Medicaid and Medicare and, 69–71, 75–76, 88, 100, 164, 179, 181–82
    private insurance plans and, 99
    seniors and, 73–78, 164, 181
household income, 29, 113, 188
Hoyer, Steny, 95
H.R. 3590, 116–17, 152
Hyde Amendment, 163
Hyde, Henry, 163

I
Illinois, 163
immigrants
    illegal, 19, 30, 167
    legal, 30
income verification, 10

Independent Payment Advisory Board (IPAB), 83–85, 120, 151, 157, 177
Indiana, 32, 68
Indian Health Care Improvement Act, 165
individual mandate, 16, 23, 57, 154, 175
Ingram, Sarah Hall, 19
insurance brokers, 25, 43, 147, 159
insurance companies, 63, 90, 99, 160, 186
　caps on payouts and, 60, 191
　taxes on, 166
insurance market, 161
Internal Revenue Service (IRS), 1, 3, 13, 25, 19–20, 36, 43, 49, 87, 91, 113, 129, 176, 184, 191
Investor's Business Daily, 54, 194

J
James Buchanan Brady Urological Institute, 189–90
Jarrett, Valerie, 56
jobs, 53–54, 58, 150
Johns Hopkins Medicine, 69
Johns Hopkins University, 189–90
Joint Committee on Taxation, 90
Journal of the American Medical Association, 79
Judicial Watch, 112, 114

K
Kavanaugh, Brett, 114
Koh, Howard, 171
Kwerling, Hayward K., 101

L
lawsuits, 106, 112–15, 128–30, 152, 155, 167, 178, 182
Leahy, Michael Patrick, 116
Lee, Mike, 110, 113

legislation, 47, 100–1, 112, 120, 135–36, 155, 165, 187, 190
LePage, Paul, 26
lethal drugs, 118
Little Sisters of the Poor, 129
lobbyists, 134
Lockton Benefit Group, 52
Los Angeles, CA, 3, 33, 99, 167
Los Angeles Community Action Network, 168
Los Angeles Times, 126
Louisiana, 190
low-income workers, 69, 160

M
Madison, James, 11, 110, 112, 118, 145
Maine, 26
Manhattan Institute, the, 31, 115
Mardel Christian bookstores, 126
Maryland, 15, 72, 95
Massachusetts, 32, 101,
Mayo Clinic (Minnesota), 33
McCain, John, 138
McDonald's, 46
McKinsey Center for U.S. Health System Reform, 34
McKinsey & Company, 2, 42, 52
"meaningful use," 20–21, 100–1
Medicaid, 17, 30, 42, 63, 75–76, 80, 84, 100, 137, 160, 177, 188
　enrolling in, 3, 23, 48, 99, 170, 172–74
　exchanges versus, 34, 43, 57, 99
　expansion of, 65–68, 71, 94
　funding for, 83
　payments of, 36, 66, 71, 98
　private insurance versus, 102
　qualifying for, 19, 22
　states and, 21, 66–67, 72, 170, 178
　Supreme Court ruling and, 154
　surgery patients and, 65, 69–71
Medi-Cal, 66
medical devices, 90, 154

medical loss ratio, 178
medical malpractice, 149, 178
medical records, 13, 20, 199, 162
Medicare, 18, 23, 30, 42, 61, 63,
    68, 72–89, 94–95, 98–102, 120,
    136–37, 151, 172–82
    Medicare Advantage, 4, 73–74,
    81–83, 162. *See also* Medicare
    Part C
    Medicare Part A, 154, 161, 179,
    182
    Medicare Part B, 179, 182
    Medicare Part C, 179. *See also*
    Medicare Advantage
    Medicare Part D, 86, 153, 172,
    179
medicine, 35, 100–3, 136, 140,
    169, 178, 193
Meet the Press, 138
Mennonites, 126
Michigan, 163
Mikulski, Barbara, 143
Miller, Edward, 69
Milliman & Robertson, 71
mini-med plans, 46, 61, 153
mini-med waivers, 47
minorities, 64, 160
Mississippi, 55
Moffit Cancer Center, 82
"morning after" drugs, 124,
    126, 170, 191. *See also*
    abortifacients; Plan B pills
Musgrove, Philip, 139

N

National Association of
    Community Health Centers,
    37–38
National Association of Medicaid
    Directors, 72
National Bureau of Economic
    Research, 76
National Committee on Vital
    and Health Statistics, 119

National Conference of State
    Legislatures, 64
National Federation of
    Independent Businesses, 49
National Institutes of Health, 165
National Steering Committee, 183
Natural Resources Defense
    Council, 167
"navigators," 25, 36–37, 39,
    180–81
NBA, 56
Nebraska, 32, 170–71
Nelson, Ben, 170
Nevada, 32, 94
New England Journal of Medicine,
    139
New Hampshire, 3, 28, 32–33
New Jersey, 32, 47, 64, 134
New Mexico, 32
New York, 3–4, 32–34, 40, 47, 64,
    68, 82, 99, 129–30, 134
New York Civil Liberties Union,
    20
New Yorkers, 148
New York Presbyterian hospital,
    3, 33, 99
New York Times, 26, 44, 126
NFL, 56
Nixon, Richard, 109
Nobel Prize, 140
North Carolina, 112
nurses, 4, 76, 137, 142, 161, 171
nursing homes, 74–75, 78, 182
nutritional labeling, 181

O

Obama administration, 6, 9, 15,
    20, 43, 45–47, 95, 101, 113–14,
    124, 126–27, 129, 153, 155, 165,
    181, 183, 187, 191
Obama, Barack, 1–2, 6, 9–15,
    22, 29–60, 93, 99–119, 127–31,
    137–38, 142–52, 170, 174

Obamacare. *See* Obama health law; Patient Protection and Affordable Care Act

Obama health law, 6, 9, 142, 152, 182–83. *See also* Patient Protection and Affordable Care Act
  Constitution and, 7, 10–11, 84, 106–10, 116, 182
  the deficit and, 93, 95
  employer-provided insurance coverage and, 1, 5, 8, 14, 16, 18, 22, 42–43, 52, 62–63, 90, 142, 144, 166, 173, 175, 179, 186, 188, 191
  exchanges of, 2–3, 22, 26–29, 33–36, 62, 99, 107, 114, 155, 171, 174–75, 183, 188–89
  expanded benefits and, 160, 178
  expansion of Medicaid and, 21–22, 68, 71, 94, 99, 160, 178
  health reform and, 14, 34, 51, 90, 95, 128, 131, 133–34, 137–39, 142, 170
  impact of, 1, 103
  individual mandate of, 16, 23, 50, 57, 111, 154, 175
  losers, 10–11, 72, 80, 107, 160–62
  Medicare and, 4, 18, 42, 63, 68–84, 88–89, 94–102, 120, 133, 137, 162–73, 177, 179, 181–82
  new taxes of, 5, 68, 71, 87–95, 186, 188
  physicians and, 34, 73, 80, 98–103, 119, 162, 172, 189
  regulations of, 2, 6, 16, 35, 46, 102, 165, 181
  tax hikes and, 5, 87–88, 94, 188
  winners, 10–11, 80, 140, 159–61
observation care, 181–82
Office of the National Coordinator for Health Information Technology, 101

Office of Personnel Management (OPM), 144, 190
Ohio, 32, 124
Oklahoma, 55, 67, 113
Open Society, 38, 106
Oregon, 118
Organization of Black Unity, 28
Origination Clause, the, 182
Orszag, Peter, 76
out-of-pocket health expenses, 10, 30, 133, 157, 182–83
over-the-counter-drugs, 91, 177

P

parental coverage, 45, 59, 61–62, 142, 148, 153, 160, 183–84
Partial Birth Abortion Ban Act, 119
part-time employment, 5, 45, 53–54, 183
Patient Protection and Affordable Care Act. *See also* Obama health law
  Section 399NN, 165
  Section 1251(a)(1), 15
  Section 1251(d), 15, 159
  Section 1302, 50
  Section 1311, 26, 35, 175
  Section 1311c(1)B, 35
  Section 1311c(1)C, 34
  Section 1311d(4)D, 35
  Section 1311(h), 4, 118
  Section 1311(h)(1), 102
  Section 1312(d)(3)(D), 144
  Section 1322, 169
  Section 1513 (Employer Responsibility), 47
  Section 2702, 156
  Section 2713, 60
  Section 3000, 78
  Section 3405, 83
  Section 4104(a), 80
  Section 4105(a), 81, 189
  Section 4201, 167

Section 4206, 181
Section 4207, 184
Section 4302, 176
Section 5000A(g)(2)(A), 18
Section 5307, 171
Section 6056, 8
patients, 6, 20–21, 35, 70, 76–79,
   82, 98–100, 102–3, 119, 135–36,
   139, 142, 160–62, 164, 169,
   173, 181
   elderly, 4, 78, 147, 181
   Medicaid patients, 34, 65,
   69–71, 102
   privately insured, 4, 34, 70–71,
   79, 97, 99, 102, 118
   and surgery, 65, 69
Payne, Grady, 55–56
payouts, 60, 191
Pelosi, Nancy, 37, 58, 152
penalties, 13, 17–20, 31, 35, 47,
   64, 91–92, 100–1, 107, 115, 117,
   125, 153, 156–57, 182–85. *See
   also* fines
Pence, Mike, 68
Pennsylvania, 163
Perry, Rick, 67
pharmaceutical companies, 86,
   90, 153
pharmaceuticals, 90–91
physical therapy, 73, 78
Physicians Foundation, 172
Pitts, Joe, 163
Plan B pills, 126. *See also*
   abortifacients; "morning
   after" drugs
Planned Parenthood, 119, 126
poverty level, 30, 66, 173, 187
pre-existing conditions, 63–64,
   147, 149, 156, 188
premiums, 10, 17, 29, 31–32, 36,
   39, 46, 50, 57, 59–62, 64–65,
   71–72, 90, 95, 99, 102, 106, 113,
   115, 117, 131, 133–34, 142–44,
   146, 148, 150, 153, 162, 176,
   178, 180, 186, 188

prescription drugs, 86, 91, 172,
   177
preventive care, 33, 59–60,
   80–81, 131, 135, 153, 176, 189
Priebus, Reince, 143
primary care doctors, 33, 71, 102,
   189
primary residence, 5, 89, 180
Princeton, 28
prisoners, 18
privacy, 19–21, 118–20, 146, 162,
   176
private insurance, 4, 6, 22, 30, 34,
   65, 69–72, 79, 81, 94–95, 97–99,
   102, 118, 134, 161, 179
pro-lifers, 128, 164
promotores, 183
proof of insurance, 1, 3, 17, 43
Pruitt, Scott, 113
PSA tests, 189–90
Puzder, Andrew, 54

Q

"qualified plan," 19, 62, 102, 175,
   184

R

Rangel, Charlie, 116
Rating Bands, 184
Ravitch, Richard, 68
Rawlins, Michael, 135
Reagan, Ronald, 109
Reasonable Break Time for
   Nursing Mothers, 184
Reformed Presbyterian Church
   of North America, 128
Regulations, 2, 6, 16, 32, 35,
   45–46, 102, 124, 154, 161, 165,
   181, 185
Reid, Harry, 94, 117
reinsurance fees, 185–86
religion, 124, 177
Religious Freedom Restoration
   Act of 1993, 125

reporting, 5–6, 8, 51, 99
Republican National Committee, the, 143
Republicans, 37, 108–12, 143–44, 149, 152, 163, 170
Rhode Island, 32
Rhode Island Medical Society, 82
Rienzi, Mark, 129
Rothstein, Mark, 20

S
Salvation Army, 54
Samuelson, Robert J., 53
Sarbanes-Oxley, 121
Scherz, Hal, 99
Schwarzenegger, Arnold, 170
Sebelius, Kathleen, 27, 37, 56, 127, 136, 160, 164, 174
Secretary of Health and Human Services, 4, 27, 35, 37, 46, 56, 80–81, 97, 102, 114, 127, 136, 160, 164, 170–71, 174, 176, 185, 189
self-employment, 58, 186
self-insured, 50–51, 90, 185–86
Senate Bill 35 (California), 38
seniors, 4, 73–87, 92, 95, 97, 137, 151,162, 164, 172, 179, 181–82, 189
Service Employees International Union, 38
Service Members Home Ownership Tax Act of 2009, 116
Sherk, James, 47
"single payer" healthcare, 72
Slovenia, 138
Small Business and Entrepreneurship Council, 186–87
small businesses, 5, 49, 56, 90, 186–87
small business tax credits, 186–87
Soros, George, 38

South Carolina, 55
South Dakota, 32
Stark, Pete, 84
State Budget Crisis Task Force, 68
State of the Union (CNN), 143
sterilization, 124, 170, 191
stimulus legislation, 20, 100–1, 109, 168, 187. *See also* American Recovery and Reinvestment Act
St. Luke's Cataract & Laser Institute, 82
stocks, 5, 89
Stupak, Bart, 163
subsidies, 3, 10–11, 19, 22–23, 29–30, 35, 48–50, 54, 64, 94, 106, 108, 113–15, 143, 145, 149, 155, 159–60, 162–64, 171, 179, 184, 187–88, 190
Supreme Court, 9, 65, 105, 110, 114–15, 118–20, 125–26, 154, 177

T
Tammany Hall, 39
Tampa Bay Times, 138
Tampa Eye Institute, 82
tanning salons, 88–90, 153, 188
taxes, 19, 37, 39, 51, 87–95, 116, 154, 174–76, 187, 191
  "Cadillac tax," 51, 87, 92–93, 157, 162, 166
  deductions of medical expenses and, 92, 179
  federal taxes, 71
  new Obamacare taxes, 5, 23, 57, 75, 87–91, 151, 153–54, 161, 180, 182, 186, 188
  proof of insurance and, 1, 3, 17, 43
  Small Business Tax Credits, 186–87
  state taxes, 68, 71
  tax refund, 3, 18, 184–85

taxpayers, 10, 26, 29–30, 48, 57, 66–68, 70–72, 81, 86–87, 95, 106–8, 144–45, 160–61, 170, 176, 178, 180, 187
technology, 100–1, 135–38, 172, 187, 194
temporary high-risk pool, 63–64, 188. *See also* high-risk pools
TennCare, 66
Tennessee, 55, 66
Texas, 37, 55, 67, 178, 181
Third World Center, 28
Treasury Notes blog, 44

U
unearned income, 89, 154, 161, 180
uninsured, 2, 6–7, 13–14, 17, 22, 25–26, 37–39, 42–43, 49, 57, 65, 145, 150, 167, 188–89
unions, 10, 15, 20, 36, 38–40, 46–47, 56, 61, 93, 128, 142, 153, 159, 161, 180, 185, 191
UnitedHealthcare, 4, 82
United Parcel Service (UPS), 45
University of Louisville School of Medicine, 20
University of Virginia, 69
Urban Institute, 52
U.S. Census, 36, 188
U.S. Constitution, 7, 9–11, 84, 106, 108–12, 114–18, 121, 128, 144–45, 152, 154, 159, 182
U.S. District Court for the Southern District of Florida, 112
U.S. House of Representatives, 9, 37, 58, 95, 108–11, 116–17, 152, 164, 182
U.S. Preventive Services Task Force (USPSTF), 80–81, 189–90

U.S. Senate, 9, 94, 110, 116–17, 120, 152, 163–64, 182
U.S. Treasury Department, 44, 87, 112
Utah, 110

V
Vermont, 32
Virginia, 55, 67, 106
Vitter Amendment, 190
Vitter, David, 190
Volcker, Paul, 68

W
W-2 form, 5, 190–91
waivers, 10, 46–47, 56–57, 61, 128, 142, 153, 170, 191–92
Wall Street, 93
Wall Street Journal, 54, 186
Washington, 72
Washington, D.C., 2, 6–7, 11, 43, 51, 55, 67, 69, 73, 82, 95, 101, 103, 125, 131–32, 134–35, 138, 143–44, 146, 175
WellPoint, 28, 33
Wetherhorn, Marc, 37–38
White House, 28, 56, 61, 124, 127, 142, 170, 174
White House Office of Health Reform, 134
White, Ronald, 113
Whitley, Toni Townes, 28
World Health Organization (WHO), 138–39

Y
young adults, 19, 153, 160, 184
Yucca Mountain, 114